180 Days of READING for Third Grade

Author

Christine Dugan, M.A.Ed.

SHELL EDUCATION

Publishing Credits

Dona Herweck Rice, *Editor-in-Chief*; Robin Erickson, *Production Director*;
Lee Aucoin, *Creative Director*; Timothy J. Bradley, *Illustration Manager*;
Conni Medina, M.A.Ed., *Editorial Director*; Sara Johnson, M.S.Ed., *Senior Editor*;
Aubrie Nielsen, M.S.Ed., *Editor*; Beth Pachal, M.A.T., *Associate Education Editor*;
Grace Alba, *Designer*; Janelle Bell-Martin, *Illustrator*; Stephanie Reid, *Photo Editor*;
Corinne Burton, M.A.Ed., *Publisher*

Image Credits

Cover Janelle Bell-Martin; p. 144 NASA/Bill Ingalls [STS-135]; p. 180, 204, 216 Getty Images; p. 228 Perdue University Libraries'/The George Palmer Putnam Collection of Amelia Earhart Papers/Karnes Archives & Special Collections; all others Shutterstock

Standards

© 2004 Mid-continent Research for Education and Learning (McREL)
© 2007 Teachers of English to Speakers of Other Languages, Inc. (TESOL)
© 2007 Board of Regents of the University of Wisconsin System. World-Class Instructional Design and Assessment
  (WIDA). For more information on using the WIDA ELP Standards, please visit the WIDA website at www.wida.us.
© 2010 National Governors Association Center for Best Practices and Council of Chief State School Officers (CCSS)

Shell Education
5301 Oceanus Drive
Huntington Beach, CA 92649-1030
http://www.shelleducation.com
ISBN 978-1-4258-0924-9
©2013 Shell Education Publishing, Inc.

TABLE OF CONTENTS

INTRODUCTION AND RESEARCH

The Need for Practice

In order to be successful in today's reading classroom, students must deeply understand both concepts and procedures so that they can discuss and demonstrate their understanding. Demonstrating understanding is a process that must be continually practiced in order for students to be successful. According to Marzano, "practice has always been, and always will be, a necessary ingredient to learning procedural knowledge at a level at which students execute it independently" (2010, 83). Practice is especially important to help students apply reading comprehension strategies and word-study skills.

Understanding Assessment

In addition to providing opportunities for frequent practice, teachers must be able to assess students' comprehension and word-study skills. This is important so that teachers can adequately address students' misconceptions, build on their current understanding, and challenge them appropriately. Assessment is a long-term process that often involves careful analysis of student responses from a lesson discussion, a project, a practice sheet, or a test. When analyzing the data, it is important for teachers to reflect on how their teaching practices may have influenced students' responses and to identify those areas where additional instruction may be required. In short, the data gathered from assessments should be used to inform instruction: slow down, speed up, or reteach. This type of assessment is called *formative assessment*.

HOW TO USE THIS BOOK

180 Days of Reading for Third Grade offers teachers and parents a full page of daily reading comprehension and word-study practice activities for each day of the school year.

Easy to Use and Standards Based

These activities reinforce grade-level skills across a variety of reading concepts. The questions are provided as a full practice page, making them easy to prepare and implement as part of a classroom morning routine, at the beginning of each reading lesson, or as homework. The weekly focus alternates between fiction and nonfiction standards.

Every third-grade practice page provides questions that are tied to a reading or writing standard. Students are given the opportunity for regular practice in reading comprehension and word study, allowing them to build confidence through these quick standards-based activities.

Question	Common Core State Standards
Days 1–3	
1–2	**Reading Anchor Standard 1:** *Read closely to determine what the text says explicitly and to make logical inferences from it.*
3	**Reading Foundational Skills Standard:** *Know and apply grade-level phonics and word analysis skills in decoding words.*
4–5	**Reading Anchor Standard 4:** *Interpret words and phrases as they are used in a text, including determining technical, connotative, and figurative meanings, and analyze how specific word choices shape meaning or tone* **or** **Reading Anchor Standard 6:** *Assess how point of view or purpose shapes the content and style of a text.*
Day 4	
1–2	**Reading Anchor Standard 10:** *Read and comprehend complex literary and informational texts independently and proficiently* **or** **Reading Anchor Standard 6:** *Assess how point of view or purpose shapes the content and style of a text.*
3	**Reading Anchor Standard 1:** *Read closely to determine what the text says explicitly and to make logical inferences from it.*
4–6	**Reading Anchor Standard 2:** *Determine central ideas or themes of a text and analyze their development; summarize the key supporting details and ideas.*
Day 5	
	Writing Anchor Standard 4: *Produce clear and coherent writing in which the development, organization, and style are appropriate to task, purpose, and audience.*

HOW TO USE THIS BOOK *(cont.)*

Using the Practice Pages

Practice pages provide instruction and assessment opportunities for each day of the school year. The activities are organized into weekly themes, and teachers may wish to prepare packets of each week's practice pages for students. Days 1, 2, and 3 follow a consistent format, with a short piece of text and five corresponding items. As outlined on page 4, every item is aligned to a reading standard.

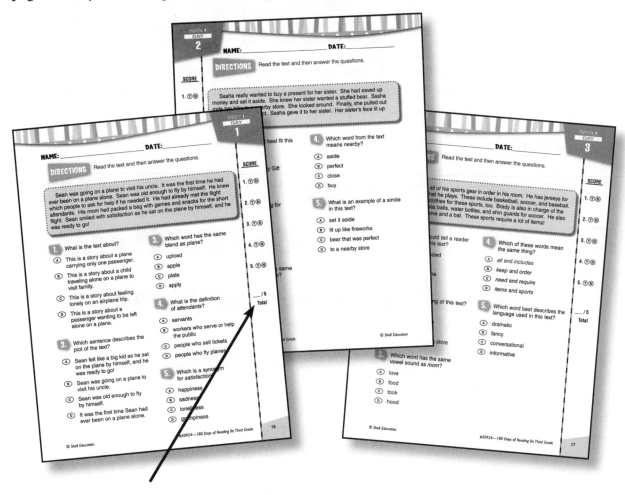

Using the Scoring Guide

Use the scoring guide along the side of each practice page to check answers and see at a glance which skills may need more reinforcement.

Fill in the appropriate circle for each problem to indicate correct (Y) or incorrect (N) responses. You might wish to indicate only incorrect responses to focus on those skills. (For example, if students consistently miss items 2 and 4, they may need additional help with those concepts as outlined in the table on page 4.) Use the answer key at the back of the book to score the problems, or you may call out answers to have students self-score or peer-score their work.

HOW TO USE THIS BOOK *(cont.)*

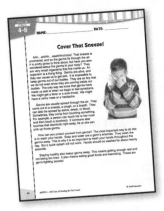 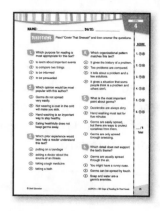 

A longer text is used for Days 4 and 5. Students answer more in-depth comprehension questions on Day 4 and complete a written response to the text on Day 5. This longer text can also be used for fluency practice (see page 7).

Writing Rubric

Score students' written response using the rubric below. Display the rubric for students to reference as they write (writingrubric.doc; writingrubric.pdf).

Points	Criteria
4	• Uses an appropriate organizational sequence to produce very clear and coherent writing • Uses descriptive language that develops or clarifies ideas • Engages the reader • Uses a style very appropriate to task, purpose, and audience
3	• Uses an organizational sequence to produce clear and coherent writing • Uses descriptive language that develops or clarifies ideas • Engages the reader • Uses a style appropriate to task, purpose, and audience
2	• Uses an organizational sequence to produce somewhat clear and coherent writing • Uses some descriptive language that develops or clarifies ideas • Engages the reader in some way • Uses a style somewhat appropriate to task, purpose, and audience
1	• Does not use an organized sequence; the writing is not clear or coherent • Uses little descriptive language to develop or clarify ideas • Does not engage the reader • Does not use a style appropriate to task, purpose, or audience
0	Offers no writing or does not respond to the assignment presented

HOW TO USE THIS BOOK *(cont.)*

Developing Students' Fluency Skills

What Is Fluency?

According to the National Reading Panel Report, there are five critical factors that are vital to effective reading instruction: phonemic awareness, phonics, fluency, vocabulary, and comprehension (2000). Rasinski (2006) defines fluency as "the ability to accurately and effortlessly decode the written words and then to give meaning to those words through appropriate phrasing and oral expression of the words." Wolf (2005) notes that the goal of developing fluency is comprehension rather than the ability to read rapidly. Becoming a fluent reader is a skill that develops gradually and requires practice. Reading text repeatedly with a different purpose each time supports the development of fluency in young children (Rasinski 2003).

Assessing Fluency

Fluent readers read accurately, with expression, and at a good pace. A Fluency Rubric along with detailed instructions for scoring and keeping oral reading records is included on the Digital Resource CD (fluency.pdf).

The table below lists fluency norms by grade level (Rasinski 2003):

Student Fluency Norms Based On Words Correct Per Minute (WCPM)			
Grade	Fall	Winter	Spring
1	—	—	60 wcpm
2	53	78	94
3	79	93	114
4	99	112	118
5	105	118	128
6	115	132	145

HOW TO USE THIS BOOK *(cont.)*

Diagnostic Assessment

Teachers can use the practice pages as diagnostic assessments. The data analysis tools included with the book enable teachers or parents to quickly score students' work and monitor their progress. Teachers and parents can see at a glance which reading concepts or skills students may need to target in order to develop proficiency.

After students complete a practice page, grade each page using the answer key (pages 231–237). Then, complete the Practice Page Item Analysis for the appropriate day (pages 10–11, or pageitem1.pdf and pageitem2.pdf) for the whole class, or the Student Item Analysis (pages 12–13, or studentitem1.pdf and studentitem2.pdf) for individual students. These charts are also provided as both Microsoft Word® files and as Microsoft Excel® files. Teachers can input data into the electronic files directly on the computer, or they can print the pages and analyze students' work using paper and pencil.

To complete the Practice Page Item Analyses:

- Write or type students' names in the far-left column. Depending on the number of students, more than one copy of the form may be needed, or you may need to add rows.

- The item numbers are included across the top of the charts. Each item correlates with the matching question number from the practice page.

- For each student, record an *X* in the column if the student has the item incorrect. If the item is correct, leave the item blank.

- If you are using the Excel file, totals will be automatically generated. If you are using the Word file or if you have printed the PDF, you will need to compute the totals. Count the *X*s in each row and column and fill in the correct boxes.

To complete the Student Item Analyses:

- Write or type the student's name on the top row. This form tracks the ongoing progress of each student, so one copy per student is necessary.

- The item numbers are included across the top of the chart. Each item correlates with the matching question number from the practice page.

- For each day, record an *X* in the column if the student has the item incorrect. If the item is correct, leave the item blank.

- If you are using the Excel file, totals will be automatically generated. If you are using the Word file or if you have printed the PDF, you will need to compute the totals. Count the *X*s in each row and column and fill in the correct boxes.

HOW TO USE THIS BOOK (cont.)

Using the Results to Differentiate Instruction

Once results are gathered and analyzed, teachers can use the results to inform the way they differentiate instruction. The data can help determine which concepts are the most difficult for students and which need additional instructional support and continued practice. Depending on how often the practice pages are scored, results can be considered for instructional support on a daily or weekly basis.

Whole-Class Support

The results of the diagnostic analysis may show that the entire class is struggling with a particular concept or group of concepts. If these concepts have been taught in the past, this indicates that further instruction or reteaching is necessary. If these concepts have not been taught in the past, this data is a great preassessment and demonstrates that students do not have a working knowledge of the concepts. Thus, careful planning for the length of the unit(s) or lesson(s) must be considered, and additional frontloading may be required.

Small-Group or Individual Support

The results of the diagnostic analysis may show that an individual or small group of students is struggling with a particular concept or group of concepts. If these concepts have been taught in the past, this indicates that further instruction or reteaching is necessary. Consider pulling aside these students while others are working independently to instruct further on the concept(s). Teachers can also use the results to help identify individuals or groups of proficient students who are ready for enrichment or above-grade-level instruction. These students may benefit from independent learning contracts or more challenging activities. Students may also benefit from extra practice using games or computer-based resources.

Digital Resource CD

The Digital Resource CD provides the following resources:

- Standards Correlations Chart

- Reproducible PDFs of each practice page

- Directions for completing the diagnostic Item Analysis forms

- Practice Page Item Analysis PDFs, Word documents, and Excel spreadsheets

- Student Item Analysis PDFs, Word documents, and Excel spreadsheets

- Fluency Assessment directions and rubric

PRACTICE PAGE ITEM ANALYSIS DAYS 1–3

Directions: Record an *X* in cells to indicate where students have missed questions. Add up the totals. You can view the following: (1) which items were missed per student; (2) the total correct score for each student; and (3) the total number of students who missed each item.

Week: _____ Day:_____

Student Name	1	2	3	4	5	# correct
Sample Student		X			X	3/5
# of students missing each question						

PRACTICE PAGE ITEM ANALYSIS DAYS 4–5

Directions: Record an *X* in cells to indicate where students have missed questions. Add up the totals. You can view the following: (1) which items were missed per student; (2) the total correct score for each student; and (3) the total number of students who missed each item.

Week: _____ Day: _____ Item #	1	2	3	4	5	6	# correct	Written Response
Student Name								
Sample Student		X			X	X	3/6	3
# of students missing each question								Written Response Average:

STUDENT ITEM ANALYSIS DAYS 1-3

Directions: Record an *X* in cells to indicate where the student has missed questions. Add up the totals. You can view the following: (1) which items the student missed; (2) the total correct score per day; and (3) the total number of times each item was missed.

Student Name: Sample Student							
Item		1	2	3	4	5	# correct
Week	Day						
1	1		X			X	3/5
	Total						

STUDENT ITEM ANALYSIS DAYS 4-5

Directions: Record an *X* in cells to indicate where the student has missed questions. Add up the totals. You can view the following: (1) which items the student missed; (2) the total correct score per day; and (3) the total number of times each item was missed.

Student Name: Sample Student								
	Day 4							Day 5
Item	1	2	3	4	5	6	# correct	Written Response
Week								
1		X			X	X	3/6	3
Total								
								Written Response Average:

STANDARDS CORRELATIONS

Shell Education is committed to producing educational materials that are research and standards based. In this effort, we have correlated all of our products to the academic standards of all 50 United States, the District of Columbia, the Department of Defense Dependent Schools, and all Canadian provinces.

How To Find Standards Correlations

To print a customized correlation report of this product for your state, visit our website at http://www.shelleducation.com and follow the on-screen directions. If you require assistance in printing correlation reports, please contact Customer Service at 1-877-777-3450.

Purpose and Intent of Standards

Legislation mandates that all states adopt academic standards that identify the skills students will learn in kindergarten through grade twelve. Many states also have standards for Pre-K. This same legislation sets requirements to ensure the standards are detailed and comprehensive.

Standards are designed to focus instruction and guide adoption of curricula. Standards are statements that describe the criteria necessary for students to meet specific academic goals. They define the knowledge, skills, and content students should acquire at each level. Standards are also used to develop standardized tests to evaluate students' academic progress. Teachers are required to demonstrate how their lessons meet state standards. State standards are used in the development of all of our products, so educators can be assured they meet the academic requirements of each state.

Common Core State Standards

The activities in this book are aligned to the Common Core State Standards (CCSS). The chart on page 4 and on the Digital Resource CD (standards.pdf) lists each standard that is addressed in this product.

TESOL and WIDA Standards

The activities in this book promote English language development for English language learners. The standards listed on the Digital Resource CD (standards.pdf) support the activities presented in this product.

NAME:_____ DATE:_____

DIRECTIONS Read the text and then answer the questions.

Sean was going on a plane to visit his uncle. It was the first time he had ever been on a plane alone. Sean was old enough to fly by himself. He knew which people to ask for help if he needed it. He had already met the flight attendants. His mom had packed a bag with games and snacks for the short flight. Sean smiled with satisfaction as he sat on the plane by himself, and he was ready to go!

1. (Y) (N)

2. (Y) (N)

3. (Y) (N)

4. (Y) (N)

5. (Y) (N)

___ / 5

Total

1. What is the text about?

(A) This is a story about a plane carrying only one passenger.

(B) This is a story about a child traveling alone on a plane to visit family.

(C) This is a story about feeling lonely on an airplane trip.

(D) This is a story about a passenger wanting to be left alone on a plane.

2. What is the setting?

(A) Sean's house

(B) a park

(C) a grocery store

(D) an airport

3. Which word has the same blend as *plane*?

(A) upload

(B) apple

(C) plate

(D) apply

4. What is the definition of *attendants*?

(A) servants

(B) workers who serve or help the public

(C) people who sell tickets

(D) people who fly planes

5. Which is a synonym for *satisfaction*?

(A) happiness

(B) sadness

(C) loneliness

(D) grumpiness

NAME:_____ **DATE:**_____

1. Ⓨ Ⓝ

2. Ⓨ Ⓝ

3. Ⓨ Ⓝ

4. Ⓨ Ⓝ

5. Ⓨ Ⓝ

___ / 5
Total

DIRECTIONS Read the text and then answer the questions.

Sasha really wanted to buy a present for her sister. She had saved up money and set it aside. She knew her sister wanted a stuffed bear. Sasha rode her bike to a nearby store. She looked around. Finally, she pulled out a bear that was perfect. Sasha gave it to her sister. Her sister's face lit up like fireworks.

1. Which title would best fit this text?

Ⓐ Saving Money

Ⓑ A Special Birthday Gift

Ⓒ Happy Sisters

Ⓓ Riding My Bike

2. What is one setting for this text?

Ⓐ a playground

Ⓑ a store

Ⓒ a restaurant

Ⓓ a birthday party

3. Which word has the same vowel sound as *bike*?

Ⓐ bit

Ⓑ type

Ⓒ tick

Ⓓ bring

4. Which word from the text means *nearby*?

Ⓐ aside

Ⓑ perfect

Ⓒ close

Ⓓ buy

5. What is an example of a simile in this text?

Ⓐ set it aside

Ⓑ lit up like fireworks

Ⓒ bear that was perfect

Ⓓ to a nearby store

NAME: _____ **DATE:** _____

DIRECTIONS Read the text and then answer the questions.

Brady keeps all of his sports gear in order in his room. He has jerseys for all three sports that he plays. These include basketball, soccer, and baseball. He has practice clothes for these sports, too. Brady is also in charge of the equipment. He has a ball, water bottles, and shin guards for soccer. He also has a baseball glove and a bat. These sports require a lot of items!

1. Which title would tell a reader more about this text?

  (A) Staying Organized

  (B) Sports Gear

  (C) Brady's Dilemma

  (D) Jerseys

2. What is the setting of this text?

  (A) a baseball field

  (B) at soccer practice

  (C) Brady's room

  (D) the sporting goods store

3. Which word has the same vowel sound as *room*?

  (A) love

  (B) food

  (C) took

  (D) hood

4. Which of these words mean the same thing?

  (A) *all* and *includes*

  (B) *keep* and *order*

  (C) *need* and *require*

  (D) *items* and *sports*

5. Which word best describes the language used in this text?

  (A) dramatic

  (B) fancy

  (C) conversational

  (D) informative

SCORE

1. Ⓨ Ⓝ

2. Ⓨ Ⓝ

3. Ⓨ Ⓝ

4. Ⓨ Ⓝ

5. Ⓨ Ⓝ

___/5

Total

NAME: _____ DATE: _____

Sending Thanks

March 10, 2012

Dear Grandma,

I wanted to write you a note to say thank you for my present. It came in the mail yesterday, the day before my birthday. I love the books! How did you know that I was reading the series on ancient Egypt? Did my dad tell you that I am interested in that topic?

I also loved the soccer clothes. My spring season starts in a few weeks, and I can wear these clothes for my weekly soccer practice. I really hope I score a few goals this season. I'm going to work really hard to try to make that happen.

When will you be able to visit me here? I miss you so much and hope we can see each other soon. I know the plane ride can be a long one, but I really hope that I see you.

Did my mom tell you that I am almost done with third grade? I have only six more weeks until summer vacation, and I can't wait for the break. We are going camping at the river. I am so excited to jump into the water with the rope swing. That is the best!

I love you, Grandma. Thanks again for my
                birthday presents.

                            Sincerely,

                            Greta

NAME: _____ **DATE:** _____

DIRECTIONS Read "Sending Thanks" and then answer the questions.

1. Think about the title. Which prediction is the most accurate for the letter?

Ⓐ A character has to say thank you but does not want to.

Ⓑ This is a thank-you letter to a family member.

Ⓒ A character sends thank-you flowers instead of a card.

Ⓓ A character tells another person thank you in person.

2. What message is the author sending to readers?

Ⓐ Summer vacation always includes camping.

Ⓑ Grandmothers live far away.

Ⓒ Thank-you notes are important.

Ⓓ Soccer is a brutal competition.

3. Who might make a connection to Greta's experience?

Ⓐ a person who loves summer

Ⓑ a child who does not like camping

Ⓒ a child who has to write thank-you notes after Christmas

Ⓓ a person who plays soccer

4. Which statement is true about Greta?

Ⓐ She loves her grandma.

Ⓑ She likes ancient Egypt.

Ⓒ She has good manners.

Ⓓ all of the above

5. What lesson could a reader learn from this letter?

Ⓐ Sending a thank-you note to a grandparent is a kind thing to do.

Ⓑ Birthdays involve lots of presents.

Ⓒ Grandchildren are spoiled.

Ⓓ Summer vacation is a time to relax.

6. What other type of text would be most like this text?

Ⓐ a biography about the president

Ⓑ a nonfiction text about ancient Egypt

Ⓒ a newspaper article about rope swings

Ⓓ a fictional story about a young girl who makes cards for her friends

1. Ⓨ Ⓝ

2. Ⓨ Ⓝ

3. Ⓨ Ⓝ

4. Ⓨ Ⓝ

5. Ⓨ Ⓝ

6. Ⓨ Ⓝ

___ / 6

Total

NAME:_____ DATE:_____

DIRECTIONS Reread the text "Sending Thanks." Then, read the prompt and respond on the lines below.

Think about a gift that someone has given you. Write a short thank-you note to that person. Make sure to include why you liked the gift.

_____

_____

_____

_____

_____

_____

_____

_____

_____

_____

_____

_____

_____

_____

_____

NAME:_____ DATE:_____

DIRECTIONS Read the text and then answer the questions.

Getting sick is part of life. Yet it does not have to happen all the time! Some people get shots to help them stay healthy. These shots are called *immunizations*. They keep the immune system healthy. This system helps the body fight illnesses. People can boost their immune systems. They do this by eating well, getting rest, and exercising.

1. Ⓨ Ⓝ

2. Ⓨ Ⓝ

3. Ⓨ Ⓝ

1. What is this text about?

Ⓐ The text is about life.

Ⓑ The text is about illnesses.

Ⓒ The text is about being apart from someone you love.

Ⓓ The text is about injuries.

4. Which word means the same as *boost*?

Ⓐ prescribe

Ⓑ improve

Ⓒ blow

Ⓓ knock

4. Ⓨ Ⓝ

2. Which title best describes the main idea?

Ⓐ Getting Shots to Stay Healthy

Ⓑ Going to the Doctor

Ⓒ How to Eat Well

Ⓓ A Mother's Advice

5. What does the phrase *fight illness* mean?

Ⓐ have surgery

Ⓑ keep healthy

Ⓒ go to the doctor

Ⓓ be cured

5. Ⓨ Ⓝ

___/5
Total

3. Which word is the root word in *healthy*?

Ⓐ eal

Ⓑ health

Ⓒ stealth

Ⓓ heal

NAME:_____ DATE:_____

SCORE

1. Ⓨ Ⓝ

2. Ⓨ Ⓝ

3. Ⓨ Ⓝ

4. Ⓨ Ⓝ

5. Ⓨ Ⓝ

___ / 5
Total

DIRECTIONS Read the text and then answer the questions.

One way to stay healthy is to get enough vitamins. Vitamins are found in healthy foods. They help our bodies work well. It is always best to get vitamins from food. A pill can also be taken. It has healthy nutrients inside. A vitamin a day can keep the doctor away!

1. Which word best summarizes this text?

Ⓐ vitamins

Ⓑ doctor

Ⓒ foods

Ⓓ inside

2. What is the main idea of the text?

Ⓐ Vitamins are only found in food.

Ⓑ Vitamins help you stay healthy.

Ⓒ Doctors want you to take vitamins.

Ⓓ Vitamins are only for adults.

3. Which word has a vowel sound like the word *pill*?

Ⓐ krill

Ⓑ dial

Ⓒ height

Ⓓ bull

4. Which word is the antonym of *away*?

Ⓐ inside

Ⓑ here

Ⓒ stay

Ⓓ taken

5. *A vitamin a day can keep the doctor away* is closely related to which popular saying?

Ⓐ It's raining cats and dogs.

Ⓑ Another day, another dollar.

Ⓒ She is in hot water.

Ⓓ An apple a day keeps the doctor away!

NAME: _____ **DATE:** _____

DIRECTIONS Read the text and then answer the questions.

There is such a thing as a good germ. Some forms of bacteria live in our intestines. They help our bodies absorb the healthy food we eat. Another type of bacteria is used to make vaccines. These shots help our bodies learn to fight illnesses.

1. ⓨ ⓝ

2. ⓨ ⓝ

3. ⓨ ⓝ

1. Which title would tell a reader more about this text?

- Ⓐ Shots at the Doctors
- Ⓑ Body Health
- Ⓒ Good Germs
- Ⓓ Flu Symptoms

4. Which two words from the text are similar in meaning?

- Ⓐ *type* and *form*
- Ⓑ *fight* and *learn*
- Ⓒ *make* and *rid*
- Ⓓ *good* and *bacteria*

4. ⓨ ⓝ

2. Which index entry would lead readers to this text?

- Ⓐ childhood vaccines
- Ⓑ helpful bacteria
- Ⓒ forms of exercise
- Ⓓ body organs

5. ⓨ ⓝ

5. Why is the phrase *good germ* interesting?

- Ⓐ because germs are alive
- Ⓑ because germs are only for doctors to worry about
- Ⓒ because germs are unpredictable
- Ⓓ because germs are usually thought to be bad

___ / 5

Total

3. Which word has the same blend as the word *absorb*?

- Ⓐ able
- Ⓑ absolute
- Ⓒ tub
- Ⓓ obvious

NAME: _____ **DATE:** _____

Cover That Sneeze!

Ahh…ahhhh…aaahhhhchooo! That sneeze is uncovered, and so the germs fly through the air. It is pretty gross to think about, but have you ever wondered about the germs in your body? They are very small organisms that live inside us. An *organism* is a living thing. Germs are alive, and they can cause us to get sick. It is impossible to keep germs out of our bodies. They are so tiny that we do not even know they are coming inside our bodies. The only way we know that germs have made us sick is when we begin to feel symptoms. We might get a fever or a sore throat. We might have a runny nose or a headache.

Germs are usually spread through the air. They come out in a sneeze, a cough, or a breath. They can also be spread by saliva, sweat, or blood. Sometimes, they come from touching something. For example, a person can touch his or her nose and then touch a doorknob. If someone else touches that doorknob right away, he or she can pick up those germs.

How can you protect yourself from germs? The most important way to do this is to wash your hands. Soap and water are a germ's enemies. They wash the germs away. This is why it is so important to wash your hands throughout the day. But a quick splash will not work. Hands should be washed for about twenty seconds.

Staying healthy also keeps germs away. This means getting enough rest and not being too tired. It also means eating good foods and exercising. These are germ-fighting secrets!

#50924—180 Days of Reading for Third Grade

NAME: _____ **DATE:** _____

> **DIRECTIONS** Read "Cover That Sneeze!" and then answer the questions.

1. Which purpose for reading is most appropriate for this text?

- Ⓐ to learn about important events
- Ⓑ to compare two things
- Ⓒ to be informed
- Ⓓ to be persuaded

2. Which opinion would be most popular with this author?

- Ⓐ Germs do not spread very easily.
- Ⓑ Not wearing a coat in the cold will make you sick.
- Ⓒ Hand washing is an important way to stay healthy.
- Ⓓ Eating healthfully does not keep germs away.

3. Which prior experience would best help a reader understand this text?

- Ⓐ putting on a bandage
- Ⓑ asking a doctor about the source of an illness
- Ⓒ taking cough medicine
- Ⓓ taking a bath

4. Which organizational pattern matches this text?

- Ⓐ It gives the history of a problem.
- Ⓑ Two problems are compared.
- Ⓒ It tells about a problem and a few solutions.
- Ⓓ It gives a situation that some people think is a problem and others don't.

5. What is the most important point about germs?

- Ⓐ Doorknobs are always dirty.
- Ⓑ Hand washing must last for five minutes.
- Ⓒ Germs are easily spread, but there are ways to protect ourselves from them.
- Ⓓ Germs are only spread through sneezing.

6. Which detail does **not** support the text's theme?

- Ⓐ Germs are usually spread through the air.
- Ⓑ You might have a runny nose.
- Ⓒ Germs can be spread by touch.
- Ⓓ Soap and water are a germ's enemies.

SCORE

1. Ⓨ Ⓝ

2. Ⓨ Ⓝ

3. Ⓨ Ⓝ

4. Ⓨ Ⓝ

5. Ⓨ Ⓝ

6. Ⓨ Ⓝ

___ / 6
Total

SCORE

___ / 4

NAME:_____ **DATE:**_____

DIRECTIONS Reread "Cover That Sneeze!" Then, read the prompt and respond on the lines below.

Think about a time when you were sick and a time when you were healthy. How were those two experiences different for you?

_____

_____

_____

_____

_____

_____

_____

_____

_____

_____

_____

_____

_____

_____

_____

NAME: _____ **DATE:** _____

DIRECTIONS Read the text and then answer the questions.

The snow was so beautiful to watch as it fell. It covered everything around us. We wondered how long it would take to melt. One yard nearby had three snowmen in it. We imagined those snowmen coming to life, just like Frosty. What would they say, and how would they sound? Winter scenes like this one are just stunning.

1. Ⓨ Ⓝ

2. Ⓨ Ⓝ

1. Which sentence gives an accurate summary of the text?

Ⓐ It covered everything around us.

Ⓑ Winter scenes like this one are just stunning.

Ⓒ One yard nearby had three snowmen in it.

Ⓓ What would they say, and how would they sound?

4. Which is a synonym for *stunning*?

Ⓐ cold

Ⓑ spectacular

Ⓒ white

Ⓓ confusing

3. Ⓨ Ⓝ

4. Ⓨ Ⓝ

5. Ⓨ Ⓝ

2. What is the main idea?

Ⓐ Frosty could come to life.

Ⓑ Winter is beautiful.

Ⓒ Snow covers everything.

Ⓓ Snowmen are cute.

5. Which sense is used in this text?

Ⓐ taste

Ⓑ hearing

Ⓒ sight

Ⓓ touch

___ / 5
Total

3. Which word has the same vowel sound as *snow*?

Ⓐ through

Ⓑ one

Ⓒ so

Ⓓ how

NAME: _____ DATE: _____

SCORE

1. Ⓨ Ⓝ

2. Ⓨ Ⓝ

3. Ⓨ Ⓝ

4. Ⓨ Ⓝ

5. Ⓨ Ⓝ

___ / 5
Total

DIRECTIONS Read the text and then answer the questions.

I wonder which season my dog enjoys the most. I know he loves summertime. He loves to race down the beach and chase the seagulls. I think he enjoys autumn and jumping in the leaves with me. Springtime means taking longer walks in the sunshine. Winter days with my dog are slow and relaxing. We stay cozy by the fire. Maybe my dog is just a happy guy all through the year!

1. Which response sounds like a good prediction?

Ⓐ I think it is about seagulls.

Ⓑ I skimmed and saw the word *dog* many times.

Ⓒ The text describes an animal enjoying the different seasons.

Ⓓ I noticed the narrator tells the story in first person.

2. Which title best describes the main idea?

Ⓐ Running on the Beach

Ⓑ A Dog for All Seasons

Ⓒ Cozy Dogs

Ⓓ Happy Guy

3. Which definition of *slow* is used in this text?

Ⓐ not fast

Ⓑ taking too much time

Ⓒ restful

Ⓓ sluggish

4. Which is an antonym for the word *cozy*?

Ⓐ warm

Ⓑ uncomfortable

Ⓒ quiet

Ⓓ tired

5. What is interesting about the narrator calling the dog *a happy guy*?

Ⓐ The dog is very unhappy.

Ⓑ It is a metaphor for himself.

Ⓒ It sounds like he is talking about a human.

Ⓓ It is the dog's name.

NAME:_____ DATE:_____

DIRECTIONS Read the text and then answer the questions.

Joshua rides his bike to work each day, rain or shine. He wears special waterproof gear so that he stays dry on wet mornings. He believes that riding a bike is a great way to start the day. The ride home gives him time to think and reflect on his day. The roads are usually quiet. It makes him wonder why more people are not riding bikes each day.

1. Ⓨ Ⓝ

2. Ⓨ Ⓝ

3. Ⓨ Ⓝ

4. Ⓨ Ⓝ

5. Ⓨ Ⓝ

___ / 5

Total

1. Which title would tell a reader more about this text?

Ⓐ Riding to Work

Ⓑ Biking Rain or Shine

Ⓒ A Biking Fool

Ⓓ Reflecting

2. Why does Joshua enjoy riding his bike?

Ⓐ because he can reflect on his day

Ⓑ because he can enjoy the quiet roads

Ⓒ because he has time to think

Ⓓ all of the above

3. Which word has the same root word as *riding*?

Ⓐ rid

Ⓑ rider

Ⓒ side

Ⓓ siding

4. Which words in the text are synonyms?

Ⓐ *wonder* and *reflect*

Ⓑ *rides* and *wears*

Ⓒ *day* and *morning*

Ⓓ *think* and *quiet*

5. What does *rain or shine* mean?

Ⓐ raining very hard

Ⓑ warm rain

Ⓒ no matter what the weather is

Ⓓ drying off after rain

NAME:_____ DATE:_____

Coming in from the Cold

The two boys knew it was time to go inside. Their fingers were almost turning blue from making so many snowballs. They had built two big snowmen and had an epic snowball fight. But now their bodies were tired and cold.

Frank and Jack were both home because school had been cancelled. The storm had brought more than three inches of new snow, and the cold temperatures had frozen much of the town's streets and sidewalks. There was no way the school bus could make it up the hill to their house. So the brothers had been able to stay home. Frank was eleven and Jack was nine, and they were very responsible. Their parents both had to go to work that day, so they made a decision to let the boys stay home alone. The Packers next door were home for the day, too, in case the boys needed any help.

The boys came in and immediately changed their clothes. It felt so much better to be dry and inside, but they both still needed to warm up. Frank suggested they make a fire. Jack thought that a fire was a bad idea. They had promised their parents to be safe while they were gone. Jack worried that a fire could grow big and get out of control. He sure did not want to burn the house down!

Finally, the boys agreed. A fire was not a good idea. Yet how could they warm up? Frank suggested turning up the heat. Jack suggested getting under some warm blankets. So that is what they did. Both boys followed their own advice.

NAME:_____ DATE:_____

DIRECTIONS Read "Coming in from the Cold" and then answer the questions.

1. Which is **not** a good prediction based on the text's title?

(A) This is a story about a person who has a cold.

(B) This story is about going inside to get warm.

(C) This story takes place somewhere cold.

(D) This story happens in the winter.

2. What is the author's opinion about staying home alone?

(A) No child should ever be alone.

(B) Children cannot make good decisions on their own.

(C) Children should not be alone at night.

(D) Children can stay home when they can follow the house rules.

3. Which statement shows a connection to the text?

(A) I hate fire drills at school.

(B) I like summer.

(C) I follow the rules in my house when my parents are gone.

(D) I had a fire when my family went camping.

4. Which word best describes Frank and Jack?

(A) tired

(B) responsible

(C) silly

(D) careless

5. Which theme applies to this text?

(A) A snowy day at home is boring.

(B) School buses cannot move very well on snowy roads.

(C) Brothers can help each other be responsible and follow directions.

(D) A fire is safe at home.

6. What type of text is this story similar to?

(A) an adventure story about two kids using a time machine

(B) a nonfiction text about snow

(C) a fictional story about making the right choice

(D) a poem about brothers

1. (Y)(N)

2. (Y)(N)

3. (Y)(N)

4. (Y)(N)

5. (Y)(N)

6. (Y)(N)

___ / 6
Total

NAME: _____ DATE: _____

DIRECTIONS Reread "Coming in from the Cold." Then, read the prompt and respond on the lines below.

Think about ways that you might stay safe when you are alone. What is one way to stay safe when you are home alone?

_____

_____

_____

_____

_____

_____

_____

_____

_____

_____

_____

_____

_____

_____

_____

NAME:_____ DATE:_____

DIRECTIONS Read the text and then answer the questions.

Sir Edmund Hillary was an amazing man. He was the first person to reach the top of Mount Everest. He did this in 1953. He was very curious about this part of the world. He returned to the area after his climb. He raised funds for small towns near Everest. This money helped people build bridges and schools. Hospitals were also built. He worked hard to make a better world.

1. Ⓨ Ⓝ

2. Ⓨ Ⓝ

3. Ⓨ Ⓝ

1. Which image would tell a reader more about this text?

Ⓐ a photograph of a school

Ⓑ a picture of money used in this part of the world

Ⓒ a chart showing the number of homes built

Ⓓ a photograph of Sir Edmund Hillary

2. Which title reflects the main idea?

Ⓐ Up to the Peak

Ⓑ The Amazing Sir Edmund

Ⓒ Building Bridges

Ⓓ Parts of the World

3. What do you think *raised* means in this text?

Ⓐ collected

Ⓑ built

Ⓒ high

Ⓓ lifted

4. What is the definition of *funds* as it is used in this text?

Ⓐ supplies

Ⓑ accounts

Ⓒ treasures

Ⓓ money

4. Ⓨ Ⓝ

5. Ⓨ Ⓝ

5. What is the author's opinion of Sir Edmund Hillary?

Ⓐ The author doubts his achievements.

Ⓑ The author respects him.

Ⓒ The author does not understand him.

Ⓓ The author is confused by him.

___ / 5

Total

NAME:_____ DATE:_____

SCORE

1. Ⓨ Ⓝ

2. Ⓨ Ⓝ

3. Ⓨ Ⓝ

4. Ⓨ Ⓝ

5. Ⓨ Ⓝ

___ / 5
Total

DIRECTIONS Read the text and then answer the questions.

Mount Everest is a tall mountain. It is on the border of Tibet and Nepal. India is nearby. There are many tall summits in the area. The ten tallest peaks in the world are there. The peaks are quite old. Mount Everest was formed sixty million years ago. It is still growing! It grows about two inches every year.

1. What topic is the main focus of this text?

Ⓐ Tibet

Ⓑ Nepal

Ⓒ Mt. Everest

Ⓓ old peaks

2. Which word would most likely be found in the glossary of this text?

Ⓐ years

Ⓑ summits

Ⓒ ten

Ⓓ still

3. Which words have the same vowel sound?

Ⓐ *grows* and *old*

Ⓑ *ten* and *tall*

Ⓒ *on* and *old*

Ⓓ *are* and *peaks*

4. Which word is a synonym for *peaks*?

Ⓐ trees

Ⓑ curves

Ⓒ mountain tops

Ⓓ plants

5. What type of text would include language similar to what is used in this text?

Ⓐ a social studies book

Ⓑ a joke book

Ⓒ a letter

Ⓓ a thank-you note

NAME: _____ **DATE:** _____

DIRECTIONS Read the text and then answer the questions.

> Mountain climbers have to wear special gear that protects them from the snow and cold. They wear a lot of layers that help them stay warm. This includes gloves, hats, and glasses. They also have to use special tools. An *ice axe* helps to break up the ice. A *regulator* is a tool that provides oxygen to climbers. They need this at the top of the peak where the air is low in oxygen. Climbers also need a radio in case they need to call for help.

1. Ⓨ Ⓝ

2. Ⓨ Ⓝ

3. Ⓨ Ⓝ

1. Which word would help a reader make a prediction after previewing the text?

- Ⓐ warm
- Ⓑ gear
- Ⓒ provides
- Ⓓ ice

2. Which image would help a reader understand this information?

- Ⓐ a photograph of a mountain
- Ⓑ a photograph of a climber wearing special gear
- Ⓒ a photograph of ice and snow
- Ⓓ a picture of a climber's face

3. Which can be added to *protect* to make another word?

- Ⓐ –ly
- Ⓑ –ed
- Ⓒ un–
- Ⓓ dis–

4. Which of these words has the root word *ice*?

- Ⓐ icicle
- Ⓑ nice
- Ⓒ rice
- Ⓓ incident

5. What is the author's purpose?

- Ⓐ The author uses facts to teach about a mountain climber's gear.
- Ⓑ The author uses jokes to make people laugh about tools.
- Ⓒ The author compares mountain climbers to rock climbers.
- Ⓓ The author uses facts to share a biography of a famous climber.

4. Ⓨ Ⓝ

5. Ⓨ Ⓝ

___ / 5

Total

NAME: _____ DATE: _____

Mt. Everest

Mt. Everest is the tallest mountain in the world. It is over 29,000 feet tall. It is in the central Himalayas. Mt. Everest is on the border of Tibet and Nepal.

People are very interested in this amazing peak. The mountain has become a challenge for some. People train to climb it, but getting to the top of Mt. Everest is not easy. The altitude requires special attention. There is not a lot of oxygen that far up. People's bodies have to adjust. Climbing takes time. Bodies have to get used to the low oxygen levels.

The Mt. Everest base camps are where climbers begin to climb. These camps are on opposite sides of Mt. Everest. They are also very high. They are more than 16,000 feet high. Climbers rest at the base camps. They pack and get their supplies ready before they begin climbing. There are other camps on the way to the peak. It takes a while to reach each camp. Climbers spend time at the camps. This is where climbers stop to adjust to the elevation.

The highest part of the mountain is called the *summit*. It is covered with deep snow. The snow stays there all year. It is very cold up there! The wind can also blow very hard. This makes the climb pretty risky. Climbers have to be really safe. Climbers have special gear. This keeps them warm. It also keeps them from falling.

Mt. Everest

There are people who work to help climbers. They are called *Sherpas*. They carry tents. They also cook food. They work at this job to support their families. Sherpas often get help from yaks. Yaks are strong animals. They help transport goods up the mountain.

Reaching the summit is an amazing feat. Not many humans are able to do such a difficult task. Sadly, not everyone survives the trek up Mt. Everest. More than 200 people have died climbing the mountain. This sad fact reminds people of the danger in climbing.

It is a dream of many to stand on the top of Mt. Everest. People claim that they feel on top of the world. It takes bravery and hard work to do it.

NAME:_____ DATE:_____

DIRECTIONS Read "Mt. Everest" and then answer the questions.

1. What is the author's purpose?

Ⓐ to be entertained

Ⓑ to be persuaded to climb a mountain

Ⓒ to learn about Mt. Everest and mountain climbing

Ⓓ to learn about climate change

2. Which statement would the author likely agree with?

Ⓐ Climbing is too dangerous to try.

Ⓑ Everyone should try to climb Mt. Everest.

Ⓒ Climbing Mt. Everest is an amazing adventure.

Ⓓ Traveling that far to climb a mountain is silly.

3. Which statement reflects a prior experience related to the text?

Ⓐ My mom trained for months to run a marathon.

Ⓑ It is snowy today.

Ⓒ I can see a hill from my backyard.

Ⓓ I saw a cat climb a tree.

4. The first paragraph of the text

Ⓐ introduces the topic.

Ⓑ describes a problem.

Ⓒ compares and contrasts two famous mountains.

Ⓓ does not fit with the rest of the text.

5. What is the main idea?

Ⓐ Mt. Everest is an amazing place, and people who climb it are brave and strong.

Ⓑ People have died climbing Mt. Everest.

Ⓒ Sherpas make the climb worth it.

Ⓓ There are two base camps.

6. Why are climbers brave?

Ⓐ because they help Sherpas earn a living

Ⓑ because they do good things for Earth

Ⓒ because climbing is a dangerous hobby

Ⓓ because they do not know what they are doing

1. Ⓨ Ⓝ

2. Ⓨ Ⓝ

3. Ⓨ Ⓝ

4. Ⓨ Ⓝ

5. Ⓨ Ⓝ

6. Ⓨ Ⓝ

___ / 6

Total

NAME:_____ DATE:_____

DIRECTIONS Reread "Mt. Everest." Then, read the prompt and respond on the lines below.

Climbing Mt. Everest is a huge task. It requires special planning and a lot of courage. Would you like to climb Mt. Everest? Why or why not?

_____

_____

_____

_____

_____

_____

_____

_____

_____

_____

_____

_____

_____

_____

NAME:_____ DATE:_____

DIRECTIONS Read the text and then answer the questions.

"Planning a birthday party is hard," thought Jenna. She could not pick which friends to invite. Jenna was having a slumber party, so her parents thought she should only have a few guests. It was hard to narrow down her list. Jenna had friends at school. She had friends on her soccer team. She had friends from summer camp. She did not know how to include everyone in one event.

1. Ⓨ Ⓝ

2. Ⓨ Ⓝ

3. Ⓨ Ⓝ

1. Which word tells the reader most about this text?

Ⓐ summer

Ⓑ friends

Ⓒ slumber party

Ⓓ soccer

4. What is the definition of *narrow* as it is used in this text?

Ⓐ slender

Ⓑ thin

Ⓒ to make smaller

Ⓓ close-minded

4. Ⓨ Ⓝ

5. Ⓨ Ⓝ

2. Which title best describes the main idea?

Ⓐ Making a List

Ⓑ A Hard Choice

Ⓒ Jenna's Day

Ⓓ Planning the Party

5. Which sentence best describes this text?

Ⓐ The text describes a funny situation.

Ⓑ The text details an event.

Ⓒ The text describes a problem.

Ⓓ The text lists steps in a certain order.

___ / 5
Total

3. Which word has the same vowel sound as *have*?

Ⓐ happy

Ⓑ haze

Ⓒ frame

Ⓓ paid

NAME:_____ DATE:_____

DIRECTIONS Read the text and then answer the questions.

1. (Y)(N)

2. (Y)(N)

3. (Y)(N)

4. (Y)(N)

5. (Y)(N)

___ / 5
Total

The class decided to make a graph. They wanted to show their favorite seasons. They made a bar graph. It had a section for each of the four seasons. The teacher helped to tally the votes. She organized the data. Then, the class heard the results. Summer was the favorite season!

1. What does the first sentence tell about this text?

- (A) The text is about a math test.
- (B) The text is about making graphs.
- (C) The text is about hating math.
- (D) The text is about geometry.

2. What is the main event?

- (A) The class made drawings of their favorite animals.
- (B) The class made graphs of their favorite seasons.
- (C) The class likes summer the most.
- (D) There is no plot.

3. Which word has the same blend as *show*?

- (A) hope
- (B) share
- (C) how
- (D) now

4. Which of the following words is a synonym for *data*?

- (A) bar
- (B) students
- (C) information
- (D) date

5. What type of text would include vocabulary similar to what is used in this text?

- (A) an encyclopedia
- (B) a book of poetry
- (C) a letter
- (D) a math textbook

NAME:_____ DATE:_____

DIRECTIONS Read the text and then answer the questions.

Joe was not a competitive kid. He did not like to win and did not like to lose. He really did not like to compete against anyone for anything. For this reason, Joe did not like most sports. He thought it was a waste of time to play with a team. He still liked to move his body and exercise. Joe decided to start swimming. It was a quiet way to exercise. There was no competition. It was just Joe in the water, moving and pushing forward.

1. Ⓨ Ⓝ

2. Ⓨ Ⓝ

3. Ⓨ Ⓝ

4. Ⓨ Ⓝ

5. Ⓨ Ⓝ

1. Which question about the text would help readers monitor their reading?

Ⓐ How do you swim?

Ⓑ How do you play football?

Ⓒ How does Joe exercise?

Ⓓ Where are swim lessons?

2. What is the main conflict of this text?

Ⓐ Swimming is too difficult for Joe.

Ⓑ Joe thinks most sports are a waste of time, but he likes to exercise.

Ⓒ Joining the soccer team is too expensive.

Ⓓ Joe missed football tryouts.

3. Which word makes a new word by adding the prefix *dis–*?

Ⓐ play

Ⓑ win

Ⓒ forward

Ⓓ move

4. Which of these words has the same root word as *swimming*?

Ⓐ swish

Ⓑ timing

Ⓒ winning

Ⓓ swimmer

5. Which simile describes Joe's experience while swimming?

Ⓐ smart as a whip

Ⓑ quiet as a mouse

Ⓒ surprising like a shooting star

Ⓓ loud as a firecracker

___ / 5

Total

NAME:_____ DATE:_____

The Pool Party Dilemma

Marco wanted to have a pool party for his birthday. He made a list of friends he wanted to invite. His mom told him that six friends would be a good number. She wanted to be able to watch all the kids safely while they played in the pool. Marco made his six invitations at home. Then, he brought them to school the next day. He handed them to each of his friends. Max, Sam, Kai, Liam, and Felix were all excited. They each told Marco that they were sure they would come. Marco gave an invitation to his final guest, Aidan. Aidan hesitated. He smiled and was clearly happy to come. Yet something was wrong. Marco was not sure what it was, but he could tell something was going on with Aidan.

That night, Marco's mom got a phone call. It was Aidan's mom. The moms talked and then said goodbye. Marco's mom came to talk to Marco. She knew what was going on with Aidan. She told Marco, "Aidan wants to come to your party. He likes you so much. He thinks you are a good friend."

"So what is wrong then, Mom?" Marco wondered.

"Aidan is not a great swimmer," Mom said. "He gets nervous in the water. He thinks he might get teased if all the boys see him scared in the water." That made a lot of sense. Now Marco understood why Aidan was acting funny when he got the invitation.

"Okay, Mom. I would never tease Aidan, especially if he comes to my party," said Marco. Marco and his mom talked and decided that they would help Aidan out during the party. The kids would only swim in the shallow end of the pool. That way, no one would know that Aidan was nervous in deeper water. Aidan could still come to the party and have a good time. The solution was a good one. Everyone was happy, and Marco's party was a success.

NAME:_____ DATE:_____

SCORE

DIRECTIONS Read "The Pool Party Dilemma" and then answer the questions.

1. What is the main problem in the text?

(A) deciding what to serve at a pool party

(B) deciding where to swim

(C) a guest who does not swim well

(D) using sunscreen at the pool

2. How would this author likely feel about friendship?

(A) Good friends buy large birthday presents for each other.

(B) A good friend makes sure a guest is happy and comfortable.

(C) Sometimes good friends tease each other.

(D) Good friends always keep secrets.

3. Which shows a personal connection to the text?

(A) I prefer to go into a hot tub rather than a pool.

(B) I have been to a water park.

(C) I had a sleepover and helped my friend who was scared to be away from her mom.

(D) My family likes cupcakes.

4. What word would you use to describe Marco?

(A) active

(B) spoiled

(C) kind

(D) annoyed

5. What is the theme of this text?

(A) No one likes a person who complains.

(B) If you can't keep up with the group, stay home.

(C) You can tease your friend if it is your birthday.

(D) Treat friends as you would want to be treated.

6. What type of text is closely related to the theme of this story?

(A) a how-to book about making invitations

(B) a cookbook

(C) an encyclopedia

(D) a poem about a friend helping another friend

1. Ⓨ Ⓝ

2. Ⓨ Ⓝ

3. Ⓨ Ⓝ

4. Ⓨ Ⓝ

5. Ⓨ Ⓝ

6. Ⓨ Ⓝ

___ / 6

Total

SCORE

___ / 4

NAME:_____ **DATE:**_____

DIRECTIONS Reread "The Pool Party Dilemma." Then, read the prompt and respond on the lines below.

Think about how Marco handled the problem with Aidan in this story. Do you think you would have done the same thing? Why or why not?

_____

_____

_____

_____

_____

_____

_____

_____

_____

_____

_____

_____

_____

NAME: _____ **DATE:** _____

DIRECTIONS Read the text and then answer the questions.

Shaun White is a famous snowboarder. He has won many contests in his sport. He won a gold medal for snowboarding. This happened in 2006. He won a race in the Olympics. He won another gold medal in 2010. Shaun has been snowboarding for a long time. He also loves to skateboard. He was a skier first. Then, he decided to switch.

1. (Y)(N)

2. (Y)(N)

3. (Y)(N)

1. Which question about the text would help readers monitor their reading?

(A) Who is Shaun White?

(B) What is a skateboard?

(C) What Olympic medal would I win?

(D) When was Shaun born?

2. Which title best fits the text?

(A) Skiing and Snowboarding

(B) Gold Medals

(C) Shaun White

(D) A Young Skateboarder

3. Which word has the same vowel sound as *gold*?

(A) fall

(B) holly

(C) gal

(D) roll

4. What is the antonym of *famous*?

(A) young

(B) real

(C) unknown

(D) funny

5. Which word describes the tone of this text?

(A) informative

(B) angry

(C) funny

(D) persuasive

4. (Y)(N)

5. (Y)(N)

___ / 5

Total

NAME: _____ DATE: _____

DIRECTIONS Read the text and then answer the questions.

1. (Y)(N)

2. (Y)(N)

Snowboarders like to take risks and enjoy the thrill of a fun ride on the snow. Many fans of the sport like to snowboard in a half-pipe, which is a U-shaped bowl. Riders can move from one side of the bowl to the other. They jump and do tricks inside the half-pipe. The half-pipe started with skateboarders. Now snowboarders enjoy it. It takes a lot of practice to do some snowboarding tricks, but it sure is lots of fun!

3. (Y)(N)

1. What does the first sentence tell about this text?

Ⓐ The text is about snowboarders.

Ⓑ The text is about going for a ride.

4. (Y)(N)

Ⓒ The text is about safety in the snow.

Ⓓ The text is about a risk.

5. (Y)(N)

2. Which chapter title would help a reader find this information in a table of contents?

___ / 5

Total

Ⓐ Doing Tricks

Ⓑ The Thrill of a Snowboarding Ride

Ⓒ Jump and Spin

Ⓓ A Fun Day

3. Which two words from the text have the same vowel sound?

Ⓐ *takes* and *fans*

Ⓑ *thrill* and *ride*

Ⓒ *ride* and *pipe*

Ⓓ *some* and *sure*

4. Which of the following is a synonym for *risks*?

Ⓐ choices

Ⓑ chances of something going wrong

Ⓒ gears

Ⓓ speeds

5. What type of text is most similar to this text?

Ⓐ a story about thrilling sports

Ⓑ a book of poetry

Ⓒ a list of directions

Ⓓ a math textbook

NAME:_____ **DATE:**_____

DIRECTIONS Read the text and then answer the questions.

People who enjoy snow sports have to be safe. Snowy and icy conditions can be dangerous. One thing that can happen on the mountain is an *avalanche*. These are rare, but they can happen. An avalanche is a quick flow of snow down a hill. Avalanches occur on very steep slopes.

1. Which type of image would tell a reader more about this text?

(A) a list of what to take on a snow trip

(B) a river

(C) a photograph of an avalanche

(D) a picture of a mountain in the summer

2. Which word from the text would most likely be found in the glossary?

(A) caught

(B) sports

(C) avalanche

(D) people

3. Which word from the text makes a new word by adding –ing?

(A) avalanche

(B) flow

(C) safe

(D) serious

4. Which of these words has the root word *safe*?

(A) safety

(B) saffron

(C) cafe

(D) sale

5. Which statement about the text is true?

(A) The author uses facts to teach about avalanches.

(B) The author uses funny words to entertain readers.

(C) The author compares avalanches and volcano eruptions.

(D) The author uses facts to teach people how to ski.

SCORE

1. (Y)(N)

2. (Y)(N)

3. (Y)(N)

4. (Y)(N)

5. (Y)(N)

___ / 5
Total

NAME: _____ DATE: _____

Hitting the Slopes

Visit any ski resort around the world. You would definitely see a lot of skiers on the slopes. You would also see quite a few snowboarders. These two sports did not always share space so happily. It took a while for people to embrace snowboarding. Today, it is one of the most popular winter sports.

Many people think that snowboarding is a recent sport. That is not true. There is evidence from the 1920s of people snowboarding. They used wood or boards from barrels. They would use horse reins or another type of tie. This would help keep the board attached to the feet. These early fans of the sport would ride through the snow.

Many years later, others were inspired to try the same thing. In 1965, a picture was taken of a skier's unique idea. He had tied two skis together. He put a rope at the front to make it easy to steer. The skier called it a *Snurfer*. He thought of it as a snow surfboard. The idea took off.

It spread more through the 1970s. More and more skiers were interested in the sport. It was hard to find a place to go and snowboard, however. Some resorts only allowed skiing. This began to change in the 1980s.

Soon after, the rest of the world began to learn about the sport. It debuted at the Olympics in 1998. It continued to catch on with fans. The younger kids who first started to snowboard became quite good. There were contests. Legends began to emerge. These athletes were at the top of the sport. They were able to do amazing things. People were captivated.

Today, snowboarding still remains popular. A lot of young kids try it. Older fans still hit the slopes, too.

#50924—*180 Days of Reading for Third Grade*   © *Shell Education*

NAME:_____ DATE:_____

DIRECTIONS Read "Hitting the Slopes" and then answer the questions.

1. Which prediction is most accurate based on the title of this text?

(A) This text is about snowboarding.

(B) This text is about skateboarding.

(C) This text is about water skiing.

(D) This text is about surfing.

2. What is the author's purpose?

(A) to compare skiing and snowboarding

(B) to share facts about the life of a famous skier

(C) to teach people how to snowboard

(D) to share the history of snowboarding

3. Which statement reflects a prior experience related to the text?

(A) I hate the snow.

(B) I took lessons and went snowboarding last winter.

(C) I played on my soccer team in second grade.

(D) I want to visit the mountains.

4. How is this text organized?

(A) a comparison of snowboarding and skateboarding

(B) chronological history of snowboarding

(C) a list of steps for how to get up on your snowboard

(D) a chronological history of winter sports in the Olympics

5. What is the main idea?

(A) Snowboarding is becoming more rare.

(B) Snowboarding is a popular sport with an interesting history.

(C) Snowboarding is too dangerous to try.

(D) Snowboarding is a secret to most people.

6. Why is snowboarding popular?

(A) Young kids try it.

(B) Older fans enjoy it.

(C) Most ski resorts allow it now.

(D) all of the above

1. (Y)(N)

2. (Y)(N)

3. (Y)(N)

4. (Y)(N)

5. (Y)(N)

6. (Y)(N)

___ / 6

Total

NAME:_____ **DATE:**_____

SCORE

___ / 4

DIRECTIONS Reread "Hitting the Slopes." Then, read the prompt and respond on the lines below.

This text describes the history of snowboarding. What are your opinions of this sport? Would you like to try it? Why or why not?

_____

_____

_____

_____

_____

_____

_____

_____

_____

_____

_____

_____

_____

_____

_____

_____

_____

NAME:_____ DATE:_____

DIRECTIONS Read the text and then answer the questions.

Anna was having a hard year because she did not have a lot of friends in her class. She was not sure why, since she knew that kids liked her, but she really wanted a best friend. "Will you be my best friend?" she asked Pam one day.

"What about Nina or Sara?" Pam asked. "They tell everyone that they are your best friends. But they say that you never play with them." Anna saw the problem immediately. She was so busy looking for a best friend that she was missing out on just being a friend to kids.

1. Y N

2. Y N

3. Y N

4. Y N

5. Y N

1. Which word would tell a reader more about this text while previewing it?

- Ⓐ kids
- Ⓑ busy
- Ⓒ friends
- Ⓓ play

2. Which title best describes the main idea of this text?

- Ⓐ Anna and Pam
- Ⓑ Finding Friends
- Ⓒ Talking to Friends
- Ⓓ An Awful Day

3. What word part could you add to the root *miss* and make a new word?

- Ⓐ *–er*
- Ⓑ *–ly*
- Ⓒ *dis–*
- Ⓓ *un–*

4. Which word is an antonym for *immediately*?

- Ⓐ closely
- Ⓑ at once
- Ⓒ later
- Ⓓ never

5. The language in the text is best described as

- Ⓐ persuasive.
- Ⓑ formal.
- Ⓒ technical.
- Ⓓ informal.

___ / 5

Total

NAME: _____ DATE: _____

DIRECTIONS Read the text and then answer the questions.

Ted wanted to learn a new sport. His brother played soccer, and his sister was a good swimmer. Ted loved to draw, but he also wanted to be better at sports. He was not sure what to do. He worried that he was as slow as a turtle, but Ted knew he had a good eye for the ball. Ted had a perfect idea! He decided to try to play tennis. He knew he would be good at tracking that ball, and he would not have to run up and down a huge field.

1. Which prediction is most accurate after previewing the first sentence of the text?

- Ⓐ The story is about learning a new sport.
- Ⓑ The story is about giving up when something is too hard.
- Ⓒ The story is about joining a football team.
- Ⓓ The story is about doing a sport to be with your friend.

2. What is the main conflict of the text?

- Ⓐ Ted's brother is better at sports than he is.
- Ⓑ Ted wants to learn a new sport but doesn't know which sport is right for him.
- Ⓒ Ted wants to become an artist, but his parents won't let him.
- Ⓓ There is no conflict.

3. Which word has the same vowel sound as *draw*?

- Ⓐ rap
- Ⓑ fog
- Ⓒ drove
- Ⓓ ran

4. What is the meaning of *a good eye* in this story?

- Ⓐ good vision
- Ⓑ talented at watching the ball
- Ⓒ smart
- Ⓓ sunny

5. What is an example of a simile used in this text?

- Ⓐ good eye
- Ⓑ as slow as a turtle
- Ⓒ a good swimmer
- Ⓓ run up and down

NAME: _____ **DATE:** _____

DIRECTIONS Read the text and then answer the questions.

Mr. Keller was always getting names confused. He was a great teacher, and all the kids loved him. He made a lot of jokes and made learning fun, but he often called students by the wrong name. "Ella, will you get that book off your desk?" he would ask.

"Mr. Keller, I am not Ella. I am Chloe!"

"Oh, of course you are," he would say, and all the students would laugh. No one minded the mix-up because being in Mr. Keller's class was a lot of fun.

1. Ⓨ Ⓝ

2. Ⓨ Ⓝ

3. Ⓨ Ⓝ

4. Ⓨ Ⓝ

5. Ⓨ Ⓝ

1. Which type of image would tell a reader more about this text?

Ⓐ a picture of Mr. Keller

Ⓑ a picture of the classroom door

Ⓒ a list of the teachers in the school

Ⓓ a calendar showing the day's schedule

2. What is the setting?

Ⓐ Mr. Keller's house

Ⓑ Ella's house

Ⓒ playground

Ⓓ Mr. Keller's classroom

3. Which word from the text makes a new word by adding the prefix *pre–*?

Ⓐ called

Ⓑ because

Ⓒ are

Ⓓ made

4. Which of these words is a form of *made*?

Ⓐ mike

Ⓑ make

Ⓒ maid

Ⓓ mode

5. Which word describes the tone of this text?

Ⓐ factual

Ⓑ angry

Ⓒ funny

Ⓓ persuasive

___ / 5

Total

NAME: _____ DATE: _____

Seeing Double

Kelly and Karen were twin sisters. They loved being together. They were very similar in many ways. They also had their own interests. In third grade, the girls were put in the same class. This had never happened before. The girls were usually in separate rooms. They were very excited.

Kelly and Karen came to school together each day with their brother, Andrew. They liked to sit near each other. They also loved to be on the same kickball team at recess. All of this meant that the girls spent a lot of time together. They did not mind, but others started to notice that the two girls were together all the time. Kids started to refer to Kelly and Karen as "The Twins." Sometimes, other students actually got the girls confused. They called them by the wrong name. Their teacher actually did the same thing one day! This bothered the girls. They began to wonder when people would see them as individuals.

The girls decided to make some changes. They asked to have separate playdates. They wanted to find a few friends of their own. It was not so bad. They always had each other at home. They got to spend a lot of time together outside of school. They also decided to try new activities. Kelly played soccer. Karen took piano lessons. They really enjoyed that.

It took some time and some work. Eventually, the two girls felt they had made some good changes. They were still best friends. They still loved each other. Yet they each had a new, separate life. Each girl found new friends. They both loved their new hobbies. Finally, kids did not call them "The Twins." They were called Kelly and Karen, just as they should be.

NAME:_____ DATE:_____

DIRECTIONS Read "Seeing Double" and then answer the questions.

1. Which prediction based on the title and picture is the most accurate?

- Ⓐ This text is about having two people wear the same thing.
- Ⓑ This text is about twins.
- Ⓒ This text is about someone who needs glasses.
- Ⓓ This text is about having bad vision.

2. What is the author's opinion about twins?

- Ⓐ Twins like to play piano and play soccer.
- Ⓑ Twins should always dress alike.
- Ⓒ Twins should be seen as two different people.
- Ⓓ Twins fight a lot.

3. Which statement reflects a personal connection to the text?

- Ⓐ I like to play the violin.
- Ⓑ It is okay to have interests different from my best friend's.
- Ⓒ My baseball coach can be mean.
- Ⓓ I sit by myself at lunch.

4. How do Kelly and Karen change in this story?

- Ⓐ They find their own interests.
- Ⓑ They lose friends.
- Ⓒ They begin arguing.
- Ⓓ They have a sleepover.

5. What is the theme of the text?

- Ⓐ Twins are lucky.
- Ⓑ Each person is unique.
- Ⓒ Sisters fight a lot.
- Ⓓ People who look alike usually act alike.

6. What other title indicates a text with a similar theme?

- Ⓐ My Best Friend and I
- Ⓑ A New Talent
- Ⓒ Standing Out on My Own
- Ⓓ A New Nickname

1. Ⓨ Ⓝ

2. Ⓨ Ⓝ

3. Ⓨ Ⓝ

4. Ⓨ Ⓝ

5. Ⓨ Ⓝ

6. Ⓨ Ⓝ

___ / 6

Total

NAME:_____ **DATE:**_____

DIRECTIONS Reread "Seeing Double." Then, read the prompt and respond on the lines below.

Kelly and Karen want to be thought of as individuals. Why do you think it is so important for all of us to be looked at as individuals?

_____

_____

_____

_____

_____

_____

_____

_____

_____

_____

_____

_____

_____

_____

_____

NAME:_____ DATE:_____

DIRECTIONS Read the text and then answer the questions.

Swimming in the ocean is fun. It can also be dangerous. The waves can pull swimmers underwater. A riptide can do this. It is also called a *rip current*. This is a strong channel of water. It can drag people away from the beach. People fight to stay above the surface. Even strong swimmers struggle. Surfers or swimmers should swim parallel to the beach to get out of a rip current. This is very important information to know!

1. Ⓨ Ⓝ

2. Ⓨ Ⓝ

3. Ⓨ Ⓝ

4. Ⓨ Ⓝ

5. Ⓨ Ⓝ

___ / 5
Total

1. Which question about the text would help readers monitor their reading?

Ⓐ How do you get sand out of your shoes?

Ⓑ How did I get this rip in my pants?

Ⓒ Why can swimming in the ocean be dangerous?

Ⓓ What do kids learn in swimming lessons?

2. Which title best fits the text?

Ⓐ Beach Fun

Ⓑ Safety in the Water

Ⓒ Playing with Beach Balls

Ⓓ Swimming in the Pool

3. Which word has the same vowel sound as *tide*?

Ⓐ film

Ⓑ cry

Ⓒ rid

Ⓓ tidbit

4. What is the definition of *drag* as it is used in this text?

Ⓐ moving slowly

Ⓑ a nuisance

Ⓒ pulling something or someone

Ⓓ effort

5. Which word describes the tone of this text?

Ⓐ warning

Ⓑ sad

Ⓒ funny

Ⓓ historical

NAME: _____ DATE: _____

DIRECTIONS Read the text and then answer the questions.

Shark attacks are scary to think about when you are at the beach. Hearing a story of an attack on the news may make people think twice about swimming. Swimmers may not want to go in the water, or they may not even want to be on the beach. The truth is that shark attacks are rare. When a shark bites a human it is usually a mistake. A shark may think it is eating a seal. Sharks do not hunt humans.

SCORE

1. Ⓨ Ⓝ

2. Ⓨ Ⓝ

3. Ⓨ Ⓝ

4. Ⓨ Ⓝ

5. Ⓨ Ⓝ

___ / 5
Total

1. What does the first sentence tell about this text?

Ⓐ The story is about scary shows on TV.

Ⓑ The story is about shark attacks.

Ⓒ The story is about going to the beach.

Ⓓ The story is about pet sharks.

2. Which chapter title would help a reader find this information in a table of contents?

Ⓐ Sharks Are Everywhere!

Ⓑ The Truth About Shark Attacks

Ⓒ Stay Out of the Water

Ⓓ Danger at the Beach

3. Which two words have the same vowel sound?

Ⓐ *seal* and *hunt*

Ⓑ *scary* and *rare*

Ⓒ *twice* and *think*

Ⓓ *beach* and *news*

4. Which of the following words is a synonym for *rare*?

Ⓐ each month

Ⓑ never

Ⓒ always

Ⓓ uncommon

5. What type of text would include language similar to what is used in this text?

Ⓐ a social studies book

Ⓑ a book of animal poems

Ⓒ a menu

Ⓓ an article about ocean wildlife

#50924—180 Days of Reading for Third Grade

NAME:_____ DATE:_____

DIRECTIONS Read the text and then answer the questions.

Pollution on the beach is troubling. Some of that trash comes from beachgoers. Throwing garbage on the sand pollutes the water because the trash makes its way into the ocean. Some of the trash actually washes up from the ocean. Pollution can come from many places. People can work together to clean up the beaches. It makes the beach a nicer place to visit. It helps wildlife there, too!

1. Ⓨ Ⓝ

2. Ⓨ Ⓝ

3. Ⓨ Ⓝ

1. Which type of image would tell a reader more about this text?

Ⓐ a list of wildlife found on the beach

Ⓑ a photograph of a fishing boat

Ⓒ a photograph of a polluted beach

Ⓓ a picture of a "No Swimming" sign

4. Which of these words is the root word of *pollution*?

Ⓐ revolution

Ⓑ pollute

Ⓒ poll

Ⓓ Polly

4. Ⓨ Ⓝ

5. Ⓨ Ⓝ

2. Which word from the text would most likely be found in the glossary?

Ⓐ work

Ⓑ pollution

Ⓒ trash

Ⓓ sand

5. Based on the text, which statement is true?

Ⓐ The author wants to teach people about keeping beaches clean.

Ⓑ The author thinks beaches are all filthy.

Ⓒ The author compares air pollution and water pollution.

Ⓓ The author uses facts to tell the history of pollution.

___ / 5

Total

3. Which word from the text makes a new word by adding the prefix *re–*?

Ⓐ visit

Ⓑ place

Ⓒ makes

Ⓓ all of the above

NAME:_____ DATE:_____

Being Safe on the Beach

A day at the beach can be wonderful. The coast is quiet and peaceful. The view of the water is very soothing. It can also be quite dangerous. The ocean is very powerful. People need to make safe choices. This will help people avoid injury out in the waves or on the sand.

There is one major way that people can be safe on the coast. They must pay attention to signs and warnings on the beach. Sometimes, a flag will wave on the beach. The flag warns people about risky conditions.

Here are the flags that people might see on some beaches:

- A double red flag means the water is closed to the public. The entire beach is closed. People must stay out of the water. This is used for severe weather or currents. Water pollution, lightning, or shark sightings nearby also will get this flag.

- A red flag means there is a high hazard. A high hazard may be high surf and/or strong currents.

- A yellow flag means there is a moderate hazard. A moderate hazard may be strong surf and/or currents.

- A green flag means there are safe conditions. This means that conditions on the beach are safe, but beachgoers should always use caution.

Lifeguards also help with beach safety. They watch swimmers and surfers. They keep a close eye on people in the water. They will even watch people on the sand who are near the waves. Lifeguards are trained to help rescue people. They know first aid in case someone gets hurt. They can also call other rescuers to help a person who is in serious trouble.

Yet not all beaches have lifeguards. Many beaches are public property. People can visit them when they choose. There is no one to stop a person from going into the water. People have to be safe for their own good. A perfect day on the beach is always a safe day on the beach!

NAME:_____ **DATE:**_____

DIRECTIONS Read "Being Safe on the Beach" and then answer the questions.

1. What is the purpose for reading this text?

Ⓐ to be entertained

Ⓑ to be persuaded to avoid the beach

Ⓒ to learn about beach safety

Ⓓ to learn about flags

2. Which statement would the author likely agree with?

Ⓐ People can behave however they want to at the beach.

Ⓑ Stay out of the water when lifeguards tell you to do so.

Ⓒ There are no rules at the beach.

Ⓓ Strong swimmers are never in danger.

3. Which statement makes a connection to the text?

Ⓐ Our car has hazard lights in case it breaks down.

Ⓑ We fly a flag on the 4th of July.

Ⓒ I stay safe at the beach by sticking close to my family and watching the water for hazards.

Ⓓ I like the color red.

4. Which information in the text is highlighted in a list?

Ⓐ who hangs the flags

Ⓑ where the flags are hung

Ⓒ what the flags mean

Ⓓ the beaches that use this flag system

5. What is the main idea?

Ⓐ Lifeguards are not properly trained.

Ⓑ The beach is a safe place.

Ⓒ Beach safety is important.

Ⓓ Flags come in pretty colors.

6. What is one way to stay safe at the beach?

Ⓐ Stay out of the water when there is a hazard.

Ⓑ Follow the directions of lifeguards.

Ⓒ Pay attention to the beach flags.

Ⓓ all of the above

1. Ⓨ Ⓝ

2. Ⓨ Ⓝ

3. Ⓨ Ⓝ

4. Ⓨ Ⓝ

5. Ⓨ Ⓝ

6. Ⓨ Ⓝ

___ / 6

Total

NAME: _____ **DATE:** _____

DIRECTIONS Reread "Being Safe on the Beach." Then, read the prompt and respond on the lines below.

There are ways to be safe when you are on the beach. What would you do if you saw a double red flag on the beach? How would you explain the flags to your friends?

_____

_____

_____

_____

_____

_____

_____

_____

_____

_____

_____

_____

_____

_____

_____

_____

NAME:_____ DATE:_____

DIRECTIONS Read the text and then answer the questions.

José had been a dancer since he was three. He had always loved to dance, but he recently started to focus more on ballet. José enjoyed the quiet way to tell a story. The music and the movement gave him so much energy. He did not listen to people who told him that boys don't do ballet. He did ballet, and he loved it. José had a mind of his own.

1. (Y)(N)

2. (Y)(N)

3. (Y)(N)

1. What is this text about?

Ⓐ having a lot of energy

Ⓑ a ballet dancer

Ⓒ being quiet

Ⓓ music and movement

2. Which is the best description of José?

Ⓐ José is not nice.

Ⓑ José loves ballet, even though some people believe boys don't do ballet.

Ⓒ José has a lot of energy.

Ⓓ José is three years old.

3. Which definition of *focus* is used in this text?

Ⓐ a point on a cone

Ⓑ clear image

Ⓒ effort

Ⓓ concentrate

4. Which of these words means the same as *recently*?

Ⓐ always

Ⓑ tomorrow

Ⓒ lately

Ⓓ never

5. What does the phrase *had a mind of his own* mean in this text?

Ⓐ José did not behave well.

Ⓑ José was torn between two hobbies.

Ⓒ José decided things for himself.

Ⓓ José could not make a decision.

4. (Y)(N)

5. (Y)(N)

___ / 5
Total

NAME:_____ **DATE:**_____

SCORE

1. Ⓨ Ⓝ

2. Ⓨ Ⓝ

3. Ⓨ Ⓝ

4. Ⓨ Ⓝ

5. Ⓨ Ⓝ

___ / 5
Total

DIRECTIONS Read the text and then answer the questions.

Phoebe loved having pets at home to love and care for each day. She had two dogs and one cat. The strangest thing was that the three of them were very good friends. Phoebe knew that cats and dogs were supposed to be enemies, but her pets were definitely not enemies. They certainly did not fight like cats and dogs!

1. Which title best fits this text?

Ⓐ Not Your Typical Cats and Dogs

Ⓑ Phoebe's Pets

Ⓒ Pets

Ⓓ Pet Friends

2. What is the setting?

Ⓐ the pet store

Ⓑ Phoebe's house

Ⓒ the dog park

Ⓓ the doghouse in Phoebe's yard

3. Which word has the same vowel sound as *fight*?

Ⓐ crib

Ⓑ tie

Ⓒ ought

Ⓓ bit

4. Which words from the text are antonyms?

Ⓐ *pets* and *dog*

Ⓑ *love* and *care*

Ⓒ *friends* and *fight*

Ⓓ *friends* and *enemies*

5. Which phrase is an example of a simile?

Ⓐ *not enemies*

Ⓑ *love and care*

Ⓒ *fight like cats and dogs*

Ⓓ *pets at home*

NAME:_____ DATE:_____

DIRECTIONS Read the text and then answer the questions.

Henry walked to school each morning with his neighbor, James, whom he had been friends with for many years. One morning, Henry met James at the corner, and they began walking. "Where is your umbrella?" James asked Henry. "The sky looks so dark."

"It's not going to rain," declared Henry. "I watched the weather report this morning."

"Don't believe everything you hear," replied James as the first drops started to fall.

1. Ⓨ Ⓝ

2. Ⓨ Ⓝ

3. Ⓨ Ⓝ

4. Ⓨ Ⓝ

5. Ⓨ Ⓝ

1. Which picture would tell a reader more about this text?

Ⓐ a picture of two cats sleeping next to each other

Ⓑ a picture of two friends wearing a baseball uniform

Ⓒ a picture of two friends playing

Ⓓ a picture of an umbrella

2. Who are the main characters?

Ⓐ Henry and his brother

Ⓑ James and his brother

Ⓒ Henry and his father

Ⓓ Henry and his neighbor

3. Using context clues, what is the definition of *report*?

Ⓐ account

Ⓑ research

Ⓒ essay

Ⓓ news

4. Which word means *declared*?

Ⓐ cried

Ⓑ stated

Ⓒ yelled

Ⓓ argued

5. What is the tone of this text?

Ⓐ factual

Ⓑ accusing

Ⓒ cautioning

Ⓓ excited

___ / 5
Total

NAME:_____ DATE:_____

A Different Kind of Princess

Once upon a time, a princess lived in a castle. She lived with her mother and father, the king and queen. She had no brothers or sisters. As she grew up, her parents began to talk to her about whom she might marry. Her marriage would be very important. This new spouse would be an heir to the throne.

Many princesses wait for the day they can marry a handsome prince. Yet this was no usual princess. She preferred her hunting clothes to any fancy dress. She wore her hair in a ponytail instead of having long waves topped with a tiara. She hated spending her days in the castle. She did not like to just sit around and do nothing. The princess always tried to find someone to take her out to the forest. She would ride a horse and feel the wind blow through her hair. She loved adventure.

On this day, the princess did not want to talk about a marriage. She was not going to marry anyone that her parents had in mind for her. She was not even sure she wanted to be married at all. Today, she just wanted to ride her horse.

She walked around the castle. Finally, she found a servant boy. She asked him to help her get a horse ready to ride. They talked a lot. The princess really enjoyed his company. The servant boy was surprised by the princess. He expected her to be snobby. He liked talking to her, too. The princess wondered why she could not spend more time with boys like him. Why did her parents only introduce her to the sons of their friends? All this princess knew was that things were going to change. She was going to spend some time with her new friend. She was going to make her own decisions. She was going to be a different kind of princess.

#50924—180 Days of Reading for Third Grade   © Shell Education

NAME: _____   DATE: _____

DIRECTIONS Read "A Different Kind of Princess" and then answer the questions.

1. Which prediction makes the most sense after reading the title?

Ⓐ This is a tale of a princess who is not a human.

Ⓑ This tale is about a princess who cannot meet a prince.

Ⓒ This is a tale of a princess who behaves in different ways.

Ⓓ This tale is set in a faraway land.

2. Which is most likely the author's opinion?

Ⓐ A story set in a castle must have a happy ending.

Ⓑ A princess with no magic is sad.

Ⓒ Princesses can look, sound, and think differently.

Ⓓ All princesses want to find a handsome prince.

3. Which statement shows a personal connection to this text?

Ⓐ I like to go on adventures, too, even if my parents hate it when I get dirty.

Ⓑ I saw a castle in a movie.

Ⓒ I have four sisters.

Ⓓ I read a book about a family that has servants.

4. Which quality of the princess makes her a *different kind of princess*?

Ⓐ She does not like wearing a tiara.

Ⓑ She does not want to get married to a prince right away.

Ⓒ She likes to talk to servants.

Ⓓ all of the above

5. Why is the theme of this fairy tale different from many other fairy tales?

Ⓐ Most fairy tales do not include horseback riding.

Ⓑ Most fairy tales include a princess who is looking for a handsome prince.

Ⓒ Most fairy tales include wicked stepsisters.

Ⓓ Most fairy tales do not include servants.

6. Which fairy tale is the opposite of this story?

Ⓐ "Cinderella"

Ⓑ "The Little Mermaid"

Ⓒ "Jack and the Beanstalk"

Ⓓ "Goldilocks and the Three Bears"

SCORE

1. Ⓨ Ⓝ

2. Ⓨ Ⓝ

3. Ⓨ Ⓝ

4. Ⓨ Ⓝ

5. Ⓨ Ⓝ

6. Ⓨ Ⓝ

___ / 6

Total

NAME: _____ **DATE:** _____

DIRECTIONS Reread "A Different Kind of Princess." Then, read the prompt and respond on the lines below.

The character in this story is not a typical princess. In what ways are you not a typical third-grader? What makes you unique and special?

_____

_____

_____

_____

_____

_____

_____

_____

_____

_____

_____

_____

_____

_____

_____

_____

NAME:_____ DATE:_____

DIRECTIONS Read the text and then answer the questions.

Rome has many famous buildings. Many are from ancient times. The Forum is one of the most famous places. At one time, it was the center of Rome. Tourists can still visit the Forum and see the ruins. They stand amid the modern city. The Pantheon is another famous building. It still stands in Rome. It was a temple dedicated to the gods.

1. Ⓨ Ⓝ

2. Ⓨ Ⓝ

3. Ⓨ Ⓝ

1. What is the text about?

Ⓐ Roman gods

Ⓑ buildings in Rome

Ⓒ modern cities

Ⓓ centers of cities

4. What is the definition of *amid*?

Ⓐ within

Ⓑ next to

Ⓒ in front of

Ⓓ far

4. Ⓨ Ⓝ

5. Ⓨ Ⓝ

2. Which best fits this text?

Ⓐ A Temple

Ⓑ Ancient Roman Buildings

Ⓒ Tourist Spots

Ⓓ The Forum

5. Which word describes the tone of the this text?

Ⓐ factual

Ⓑ silly

Ⓒ funny

Ⓓ comparing

___ / 5

Total

3. Which word has the same vowel sound as *Rome*?

Ⓐ most

Ⓑ one

Ⓒ ruins

Ⓓ modern

NAME: _____ DATE: _____

DIRECTIONS Read the text and then answer the questions.

1. Ⓨ Ⓝ

2. Ⓨ Ⓝ

    The ancient Romans invented many things that are still in use today. One thing that came from Roman times is our calendar. The first calendar in Rome was based on lunar months. It confused people. Caesar asked for a new one. It had 365 days in a year. There is an extra day in February every four years. It is called a *leap day*. We still use this calendar today.

3. Ⓨ Ⓝ

4. Ⓨ Ⓝ

5. Ⓨ Ⓝ

1. What does the first sentence tell about this text?

  Ⓐ The text is about ancient Roman inventions.

  Ⓑ The text is about how to be an inventor.

  Ⓒ The text is about using something for a long time.

  Ⓓ The text is about visiting Rome.

___ / 5
Total

2. Which image would help a reader understand this text?

  Ⓐ a map of America

  Ⓑ a picture of a valentine

  Ⓒ a photograph of an old calendar

  Ⓓ a list of February holidays

3. Which two words from the text have the same vowel sound?

  Ⓐ *leap* and *makes*

  Ⓑ *thing* and *year*

  Ⓒ *day* and *based*

  Ⓓ *from* and *four*

4. Which has the same root word as *invented*?

  Ⓐ vent

  Ⓑ inventor

  Ⓒ invite

  Ⓓ provide

5. What other type of text is most similar to this text?

  Ⓐ a history book

  Ⓑ a book of poetry

  Ⓒ a menu

  Ⓓ a thank-you note

NAME: _____ DATE: _____

DIRECTIONS Read the text and then answer the questions.

Water was important to ancient Romans. Rome gets very hot. People needed water to stay cool. Many Romans also liked to be clean. They used clean water to bathe. Romans built a good water system. Some homes even had fresh water inside. Towns were often built near a clean water supply.

1. (Y)(N)

2. (Y)(N)

1. Which question about the text would help readers monitor their reading?

(A) How hot is it in Greece?

(B) What can I drink for lunch?

(C) How did Romans use fresh water?

(D) Where is the hottest place on Earth?

2. Which index entry would help a reader find this information?

(A) water in ancient Rome

(B) town names

(C) city government

(D) all of the above

3. Which word makes a new word by adding the prefix re–?

(A) water

(B) hot

(C) inside

(D) built

4. Which word has the root word *supply*?

(A) apply

(B) supplier

(C) suppose

(D) puppy

3. (Y)(N)

4. (Y)(N)

5. (Y)(N)

5. Which statement about the text is true?

(A) The author uses facts to teach about how to bathe.

(B) The author uses funny statements to make people laugh about clean water.

(C) The author compares baths and showers.

(D) The author uses facts to teach about ancient Rome's water supply.

___/5
Total

NAME:_____ DATE:_____

Julius Caesar

Julius Caesar is an important person in history. He was a leader during ancient times. He lived in ancient Rome. Caesar was born in 100 BC. He grew up in a simple home. His family belonged to an old Roman family. They were not rich or poor.

Most boys like Caesar did not go to school. They had tutors. Caesar had a tutor, too. He learned a lot from his tutor. He learned to read and write Latin. He also became a good public speaker. These skills would help him later in life.

Caesar fell in love with a girl named Cornelia. They were married. They had a daughter. They all lived together in Rome. He rose to power as time went on. He was given important jobs. People started to see him as a leader.

Caesar had joined the army at a young age. He quickly became a leader in the army. The troops liked him a lot. People respected him. They also started to pay attention to him. He won many battles for Rome. The Roman army was very powerful. Having the respect of that army was a very big deal.

Back in Rome, the leaders were in trouble. The republic was in shambles. Leaders were arguing. Finally, the Senate was forced to change. Three men took over as leaders. One was Caesar. Soon after, Caesar was fighting for power. He took over as the only leader of Rome. He made himself a dictator. This made people upset. Romans did not want a king. A dictator was too much like a king. They did not want Caesar to change their lives too much. Some members of the Senate decided to kill Caesar. He was stabbed to death. The day he was killed is known as the *Ides of March*.

Many men ruled over Rome after Caesar. Some were good leaders. Some were not. The Roman Empire changed a lot over the years. Caesar will always be remembered. He was an important leader.

NAME:_____ **DATE:**_____

DIRECTIONS Read "Julius Caesar" and then answer the questions.

1. What is the purpose for reading this text?

(A) to read a biography of Julius Caesar

(B) to be entertained by facts about Roman life

(C) to learn about Roman army strategies

(D) to learn how to be a good leader

2. Which statement would the author likely agree with?

(A) Caesar should have never gotten married.

(B) Caesar was a brave leader who tried to get too much power for himself.

(C) Caesar was a better soldier than a leader.

(D) Caesar didn't know how to lead.

3. Who did Caesar fight for power?

(A) Cornelia

(B) his tutor

(C) the Roman army

(D) the two other men who were also leaders

4. How is this text organized?

(A) as a comparison of Julius Caesar and Cornelia

(B) as a chronological history of Julius Caesar's life

(C) as a list of steps for how to join the army

(D) as a chronological history of Roman battles

5. What alternative title reflects the main idea of the text?

(A) The Leader of the Army

(B) The Success and Struggles of Julius Caesar

(C) A Smart Marriage

(D) Betrayed by the Man

6. What mistake led to Caesar's death?

(A) He did not know how to lead.

(B) He was not smart enough.

(C) The army did not respect him.

(D) He tried to have too much power and made too many enemies.

1. (Y)(N)

2. (Y)(N)

3. (Y)(N)

4. (Y)(N)

5. (Y)(N)

6. (Y)(N)

___ / 6

Total

NAME:_____ DATE:_____

SCORE

___ / 4

DIRECTIONS Reread "Julius Caesar." Then, read the prompt and respond on the lines below.

Julius Caesar had a life full of ups and downs. Do you think he was a smart leader? Why or why not?

_____

_____

_____

_____

_____

_____

_____

_____

_____

_____

_____

_____

_____

_____

_____

NAME:_____ DATE:_____

DIRECTIONS Read the text and then answer the questions.

It is not easy living in space. I miss the feeling of grass on my feet and sun on my skin. I wish that I felt comfortable with the others on this ship. It is hard to have any loyalty for any nation. Life has been hard since the Nations War in 2430. No one knows what the future holds. I just hope that some day I can go home to Earth.

1. Ⓨ Ⓝ

2. Ⓨ Ⓝ

3. Ⓨ Ⓝ

1. Which word would tell a reader the most about this text while previewing it?

Ⓐ grass

Ⓑ space

Ⓒ home

Ⓓ ship

4. What does *sun* mean in the text?

Ⓐ warmth from sunrays

Ⓑ a male child

Ⓒ a large star

Ⓓ expose something to rays

4. Ⓨ Ⓝ

5. Ⓨ Ⓝ

2. Which clue(s) tells you that this text takes place in the future?

Ⓐ It takes place on a space ship.

Ⓑ The year 2430 is mentioned.

Ⓒ It talks about the future.

Ⓓ all of the above

5. What does the phrase *the future holds* mean?

Ⓐ magical powers

Ⓑ holding a globe

Ⓒ the solar system

Ⓓ what will happen in the future

___ / 5
Total

3. Which word has the same vowel sound as *hard*?

Ⓐ hare

Ⓑ air

Ⓒ tort

Ⓓ recharge

NAME:_____ DATE:_____

DIRECTIONS Read the text and then answer the questions.

The animals in the forest were meeting. They wanted to discuss the newest resident. They were not sure if they trusted this fox. He moved into the neighborhood very quietly. He kept to himself. He seemed to be alone. What was he trying to do? The animals were going to get to the bottom of it.

1. What is true about a story that has animal characters who act like humans?

Ⓐ It will be funny.

Ⓑ It must be nonfiction.

Ⓒ It is a fantasy story.

Ⓓ It will have good and bad animals.

2. Which title best fits this text?

Ⓐ The Neighborhood

Ⓑ Fox on the Run

Ⓒ An Animal Meeting

Ⓓ Alone Time

3. Using context clues from the text, which word means the same as *newest*?

Ⓐ recent

Ⓑ resend

Ⓒ recant

Ⓓ restart

4. Which word is a synonym for *discuss*?

Ⓐ explain

Ⓑ command

Ⓒ argue

Ⓓ talk about

5. What does the phrase *get to the bottom of it* mean in the text?

Ⓐ burrow

Ⓑ find out more

Ⓒ hide

Ⓓ look underneath

#50924—180 Days of Reading for Third Grade

© Shell Education

NAME:_____ **DATE:**_____

DIRECTIONS Read the text and then answer the questions.

The six aliens landed on the mountain and left the spaceship. They were on a mission. *What is essential to life on Earth?* That was the question they were trying to answer. The leaders on their home planet were trying to find out. The aliens tried to work in secret. Little did they know that they had landed right next to a campground full of people.

1. Which picture would tell a reader more about this text?

Ⓐ a picture of an alien

Ⓑ a picture of a tent

Ⓒ a picture of Earth

Ⓓ a picture of a mountain

2. What is the setting?

Ⓐ a spaceship

Ⓑ a campground on a mountain

Ⓒ another planet

Ⓓ a home

3. Which word begins with the same blend as *planet*?

Ⓐ patter

Ⓑ splatter

Ⓒ pattern

Ⓓ platter

4. Which of these words means the opposite of *essential*?

Ⓐ basic

Ⓑ required

Ⓒ unnecessary

Ⓓ living

5. Where do you think this paragraph would fit within a longer text?

Ⓐ at the end

Ⓑ at the beginning

Ⓒ in the middle

Ⓓ It is the entire text.

1. Ⓨ Ⓝ

2. Ⓨ Ⓝ

3. Ⓨ Ⓝ

4. Ⓨ Ⓝ

5. Ⓨ Ⓝ

___ / 5

Total

NAME: _____ DATE: _____

A Magical Discovery Time

From a young age, Chester knew he was different. He had a feeling inside that he had special powers. Chester knew this, yet he decided to keep it a secret. He was not sure how his family would feel or whether his friends would understand. Kids do not always want to feel different from others, and Chester was no exception.

The first clue came when he was four years old. He was playing in his sandbox in the backyard when he saw a beautiful butterfly in the sand. He put it on his hand. Then he realized the butterfly was dead. Chester felt so sad about the butterfly that he began to cry, and his tears started to fall down his face. A tear fell on the butterfly and, in an instant, the butterfly came to life! Chester could not believe his eyes.

Another time, when Chester was five years old, he decided to climb a tree. He climbed so high that he felt stuck. He was not sure how to get down. He suddenly had the urge to let go of the branch and see what would happen. Chester was amazed. He sailed gently through the breeze and flew right down to the ground. Chester flew! He wondered what other secret powers he might have.

It took Chester years to figure out what made him special. By the time he was eight, he knew all of his powers. He could bring things back to life, he could fly, he could see through walls, and he could hear things from a great distance. These skills excited him. Yet he also felt very alone. No one else could know about these powers. He didn't know anyone else who had them. Then one day, he walked into his third-grade classroom. He was early. He was the first student there. Then, Fiona walked in. She seemed to appear out of nowhere. When she came in the room, she stopped and looked at the wall. "I guess Room 215 has a substitute teacher today," she said. Chester stopped in his tracks. How did she know that? Room 215 was next door. Could Fiona see through the wall? He was puzzled. Then he saw the smile on Fiona's face as she stared at him. He knew he had found a partner in magic.

NAME: _____ DATE: _____

DIRECTIONS Read "A Magical Discovery Time" and then answer the questions.

1. Which prediction makes sense after reading the title?

Ⓐ This story must have a happy ending.

Ⓑ This story includes magic.

Ⓒ This story happens during a single day.

Ⓓ This story takes place at the circus.

2. What is the author's purpose?

Ⓐ to compare Chester and Fiona

Ⓑ to engage readers and have them use their imaginations

Ⓒ to teach readers how to use magic

Ⓓ to explain about substitute teachers

3. Who might have the closest connection to this text?

Ⓐ a third-grader who likes to fly in airplanes

Ⓑ a child who often feels different and alone but suddenly finds a good friend

Ⓒ a person who does not believe in magic

Ⓓ an adult with very good vision

4. How does Chester feel about his magical powers?

Ⓐ He feels lucky.

Ⓑ He feels excited but also alone.

Ⓒ He feels frightened.

Ⓓ He feels special.

5. Which theme applies to this text?

Ⓐ Keeping secrets can keep you safe.

Ⓑ Having a friend makes life less lonely.

Ⓒ Grown-ups do not understand kids.

Ⓓ Substitute teachers are horrible.

6. What other type of text is similar to this one?

Ⓐ a fantasy about aliens

Ⓑ a how–to book on magic

Ⓒ a realistic fiction story about being different and finding friendship

Ⓓ a nonfiction adventure

1. Ⓨ Ⓝ

2. Ⓨ Ⓝ

3. Ⓨ Ⓝ

4. Ⓨ Ⓝ

5. Ⓨ Ⓝ

6. Ⓨ Ⓝ

___ / 6

Total

NAME:_____ **DATE:**_____

SCORE

___ / 4

DIRECTIONS Reread "A Magical Good Time." Then, read the prompt and respond on the lines below.

Think about the special powers that Chester has and is able to use. What is a super-power you would like to have? What would you do with your power?

_____

_____

_____

_____

_____

_____

_____

_____

_____

_____

_____

_____

_____

_____

_____

NAME: _____ **DATE:** _____

DIRECTIONS Read the text and then answer the questions.

> An *atlas* is a book of maps that may show countries or cities. The maps are often shown on a grid. A grid of lines is put over each map, and the lines form cells. The *cells* are labeled with letters and numbers. People can use these letters and numbers to find exact locations on the map.

1. Ⓨ Ⓝ

2. Ⓨ Ⓝ

3. Ⓨ Ⓝ

1. Which question about the text would help readers monitor their reading?

Ⓐ What numbers are in my address?

Ⓑ What letters are in my name?

Ⓒ What book did I get from the library?

Ⓓ What is inside an atlas?

2. Which title best fits the text?

Ⓐ Finding Locations

Ⓑ Letters and Numbers

Ⓒ All About Atlases

Ⓓ Map with Cells

3. Which word has the same vowel sound as *grid*?

Ⓐ love

Ⓑ fin

Ⓒ time

Ⓓ grief

4. What is the definition of *cells* as it is used in this text?

Ⓐ basic unit of living things

Ⓑ small rooms

Ⓒ producing electricity

Ⓓ the space in a table or grid

5. Which word describes the tone of this text?

Ⓐ factual

Ⓑ angry

Ⓒ funny

Ⓓ persuasive

4. Ⓨ Ⓝ

5. Ⓨ Ⓝ

___ / 5

Total

NAME:_____ DATE:_____

DIRECTIONS Read the text and then answer the questions.

A person who makes maps is called a *cartographer*. Cartographers used to draw maps by hand. Today, people use computers to draw maps. Cartographers have to change maps often. Borders move. Places change. Some countries even get new names! Maps have to be updated constantly.

1. What does the first sentence tell about this text?

- (A) It is about cartographers.
- (B) It is about road maps.
- (C) It is about carts.
- (D) It is about shopping carts.

2. Which title best fits this text?

- (A) Borders
- (B) Computer Work
- (C) Changing Names
- (D) A Cartographer's Job

3. Which two words from the text have the same vowel sound?

- (A) *maps* and *makes*
- (B) *done* and *move*
- (C) *maps* and *have*
- (D) *be* and *get*

4. Which word is a synonym for *constantly*?

- (A) each month
- (B) never
- (C) always
- (D) every day

5. What type of text would include language similar to what is used in this text?

- (A) a math book
- (B) a book of poetry
- (C) a letter
- (D) a social studies textbook

NAME: _____ **DATE:** _____

DIRECTIONS Read the text and then answer the questions.

People often think of street maps when they talk about maps. Yet there are many different kinds of maps. One type is a *population map*. It shows the number of people who live in an area. A *land use map* is another type. It shows how an area of land is divided by use. Each section of the map is coded to show how it is used.

1. Which type of image would tell a reader more about this text?

- (A) a list of what is on a map
- (B) an example of a population map and a land use map
- (C) a photograph of a cartographer
- (D) a picture of a street sign

2. Which index entry would help a reader find this information?

- (A) population maps
- (B) land use maps
- (C) maps
- (D) all of the above

3. Which word from the text makes a new word by adding the blend *sh–*?

- (A) are
- (B) used
- (C) maps
- (D) map

4. Which of these words is a form of *divided*?

- (A) video
- (B) division
- (C) vided
- (D) voided

5. Which statement about the text is true?

- (A) The author uses facts to teach about maps.
- (B) The author uses jokes to make people laugh about maps.
- (C) The author compares maps and compasses.
- (D) The author uses facts to tell the history of maps.

1. Ⓨ Ⓝ

2. Ⓨ Ⓝ

3. Ⓨ Ⓝ

4. Ⓨ Ⓝ

5. Ⓨ Ⓝ

___ / 5
Total

NAME: _____ DATE: _____

Navigating with Maps

A map is a detailed image of an area. Maps show us where things are, and they also show us how to get somewhere. They show places that are large and small. There are maps of buildings and parks. There are maps of the entire world. All maps show a large area as a small drawing.

Maps are much smaller than the areas they represent. Maps have *scales*. These show how the distance on a map relates to the real distance. Some maps have scales written as a *ratio*. It shows how one length compares to another length. An inch on a map might equal a certain number of feet or miles on land.

Maps include symbols for real things. The symbols depend on what the map is showing. For example, a large map of a state or country might have symbols for cities, highways, and rivers. A smaller map of a town may have symbols for hospitals, schools, and libraries. These symbols are all listed in one part of the map. It is called the key. The *key* shows each symbol and what it stands for on the map.

People have been using maps for thousands of years. At one time, people used only paper maps. They would have to carry the map around if they were using it to find places. Today, people use a computerized type of map. It is called a *global positioning system*. A GPS uses satellites that orbit Earth. They send signals to GPS receivers. It can show location, speed, and direction. Instead of a paper map, people use GPS receivers. A map shows up on a screen. The map will point people in the right direction by showing the route as you move along.

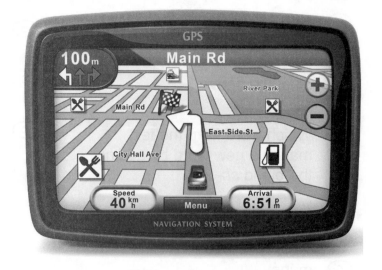

GPS receivers are also found on ships and airplanes. They help pilots and captains navigate as they travel. They show distance between locations. GPS is used with many other instruments.

NAME:_____ DATE:_____

DIRECTIONS Read "Navigating with Maps" and then answer the questions.

SCORE

1. What is the purpose for reading this text?

Ⓐ to be entertained

Ⓑ to be persuaded to buy a map

Ⓒ to learn about maps and GPS

Ⓓ to learn about direction

2. Which statement would the author likely agree with?

Ⓐ Maps are only for people who need to go places.

Ⓑ Maps are better than GPS receivers.

Ⓒ Maps are not useful.

Ⓓ Maps may look different but have the same purpose.

3. Which statement shows a prior experience related to the text?

Ⓐ I don't think maps are helpful.

Ⓑ I am curious about how keys unlock doors.

Ⓒ I want to be a pilot when I grow up.

Ⓓ I used a map to help my dad find my friend's house.

4. The fourth paragraph would work best in a _____ book.

Ⓐ history

Ⓑ art

Ⓒ math

Ⓓ how-to

5. What is the main idea?

Ⓐ Maps are interesting, and they change over time.

Ⓑ Maps do not always tell you what you need to know.

Ⓒ Maps are made by pilots.

Ⓓ A GPS receiver is not a map.

6. Why do maps have to change?

Ⓐ because map companies want to make money

Ⓑ because the world is changing

Ⓒ so that cartographers can keep their jobs

Ⓓ because maps are usually wrong

1. Ⓨ Ⓝ

2. Ⓨ Ⓝ

3. Ⓨ Ⓝ

4. Ⓨ Ⓝ

5. Ⓨ Ⓝ

6. Ⓨ Ⓝ

___ / 6

Total

SCORE

___ / 4

NAME: _____ **DATE:** _____

Reread "Navigating with Maps." Then, read the prompt and respond on the lines below.

Maps are important tools that are used by many different kinds of people. When have you used a map or seen someone else use a map? How has a map helped you?

_____

_____

_____

_____

_____

_____

_____

_____

_____

_____

_____

_____

_____

_____

NAME: _____ **DATE:** _____

DIRECTIONS Read the text and then answer the questions.

Lucy was a friendly martian. She always made sure to smile at Earthlings. She would never hurt anyone. She liked to have fun and be silly, but she would not scare someone. It was difficult to be a nice martian. All martians were thought to be dangerous and scary. Lucy had to convince everyone that she was different.

SCORE

1. Ⓨ Ⓝ

2. Ⓨ Ⓝ

3. Ⓨ Ⓝ

4. Ⓨ Ⓝ

5. Ⓨ Ⓝ

___ / 5

Total

1. What is the text about?

Ⓐ This is a story about someone being afraid of a martian.

Ⓑ It is a story about a nice martian.

Ⓒ It is a story about why martians are never nice.

Ⓓ This is a story about how to draw a martian.

2. What is the main conflict?

Ⓐ Lucy doesn't want to be a martian anymore.

Ⓑ Lucy is scared of the martians she meets.

Ⓒ Most people think martians are dangerous and scary, but Lucy wants to convince everyone she is friendly.

Ⓓ No one believes Lucy is a martian.

3. Which blend would **not** make a new word when added to *all*?

Ⓐ *sh–*

Ⓑ *sm–*

Ⓒ *ch–*

Ⓓ *st–*

4. What is the definition of *convince*?

Ⓐ explain slowly and carefully

Ⓑ to persuade someone to do something

Ⓒ break up an argument

Ⓓ work together

5. What other type of text is most similar to this text?

Ⓐ a poem about scaring your friends

Ⓑ a mystery novel about ghosts

Ⓒ a history book

Ⓓ an essay about making friends

NAME: _____ DATE: _____

SCORE

DIRECTIONS   Read the text and then answer the questions.

1. Ⓨ Ⓝ

2. Ⓨ Ⓝ

   The scientist had built the robot. Now he was not sure what to do about it. The robot was getting smarter each day. How did this happen? The scientist had checked his programming. It was as if the robot were developing a brain. He was beginning to outsmart the scientist. This was a very scary thought indeed.

3. Ⓨ Ⓝ

4. Ⓨ Ⓝ

5. Ⓨ Ⓝ

___ / 5
Total

1. Which title best fits the text?

Ⓐ A Very Smart Robot

Ⓑ A Scientist's Dream

Ⓒ A New Brain

Ⓓ Not Too Smart

2. What is the main problem?

Ⓐ The scientist could not make another robot.

Ⓑ The robot was going to hurt the scientist.

Ⓒ The scientist built a robot that was becoming too smart.

Ⓓ The scientist needed new parts for the robot.

3. Which word has the same vowel sound as *scary*?

Ⓐ fare

Ⓑ stain

Ⓒ take

Ⓓ score

4. Which of the following is a definition for *outsmart*?

Ⓐ walk outside

Ⓑ become smarter than someone

Ⓒ be smarter than your mother or father

Ⓓ doing something smart outside

5. Which phrase shows that the narrator is surprised?

Ⓐ *checked his programming*

Ⓑ *the robot was developing a brain*

Ⓒ *How did this happen?*

Ⓓ *a very scary thought*

NAME:_____ DATE:_____

DIRECTIONS Read the text and then answer the questions.

"What is that?" Brad wondered. He spotted the odd car in front of his house, but it was not like any other car he had ever seen. He walked over to the car. It did not even have a steering wheel. Instead, it had a digital calendar inside. Brad considered that it might be a time machine. He found the year 1900 and pushed the button. The car took off in the air, and Brad was off on an adventure.

1. Ⓨ Ⓝ

2. Ⓨ Ⓝ

3. Ⓨ Ⓝ

1. Which word or phrase summarizes the topic of the text?

Ⓐ steering wheel

Ⓑ button

Ⓒ time machine

Ⓓ calendar

4. Which of these words are synonyms?

Ⓐ *spotted* and *found*

Ⓑ *odd* and *adventure*

Ⓒ *wondered* and *off*

Ⓓ *front* and *seen*

4. Ⓨ Ⓝ

5. Ⓨ Ⓝ

2. Which title best describes the main idea of this text?

Ⓐ No Way to Steer

Ⓑ Traveling Through Time

Ⓒ Underwater Adventure

Ⓓ An Odd Button

5. What other type of text would use language similar to this text?

Ⓐ an instruction manual for a car

Ⓑ a biography

Ⓒ an adventure novel

Ⓓ a book about clocks

___ / 5

Total

3. Which word has the same vowel sound as *air*?

Ⓐ around

Ⓑ share

Ⓒ tack

Ⓓ aim

NAME: _____ DATE: _____

The War in Space

The Rebels were fighting the Royal Guard. It was a bad war. This was probably the worst battle in 100 years. Wars used to be fought on the ground. People used tanks and guns. Now, life had moved to space. People were setting up colonies, and no one could agree on one ruler. Two groups were fighting with spacecraft. The Rebels were not happy with the Royal Guard. They thought their leader was evil. The Rebels were trying to restore good in the galaxy.

These young fighters did not even remember another type of war. They were all born in space. Their lives took place in a large spacecraft. Entire cities could live on them. The spacecraft traveled through the darkness of outer space. It was quiet in space, and things were still. It helped keep people calm so they could forget about the past. All the survivors wanted to go back to life on Earth, but it was impossible. Earth would never be the same again.

As the Rebels fought, people followed the news on the screens. They could see which fighter planes were still out to battle and which had come back safe and sound. The Rebels were winning. Maybe there was a chance after all.

The Royal Guard began to retreat. They flew away from the battle, leaving the Rebels and their supporters to celebrate. That battle was a victory! The next step was to take back control of the colonies. The Rebels wanted an honest, trusting leader. They were willing to fight to the end to make that happen.

NAME:_____ **DATE:**_____

DIRECTIONS Read "The War in Space" and then answer the questions.

1. Which is the best summary of the text?

(A) There is a war among students over playground space.

(B) A war takes place in space.

(C) A war occurs over who travels to space first.

(D) Two countries fight over visiting the Space Station.

2. Who is trying to restore good for the people in space?

(A) the people

(B) the leader of the Royal Guard

(C) the Rebels

(D) the Royal Guard

3. Who could make a connection to the Rebels?

(A) a teacher who is trying to teach students about historical events

(B) a child who wants to join a karate class

(C) a child who is disappointed with a new, mean principal who changes the rules

(D) a pilot who is curious about space flight

4. Which statement about the Rebels is true?

(A) They are winning the fight.

(B) They are trying to restore good in the galaxy.

(C) They are fighting the Royal Guard.

(D) all of the above

5. What is a theme of this text?

(A) Be safe in space.

(B) Pay attention to authority, even if you disagree.

(C) Find a good group of people to help you in life.

(D) Fight for what you believe in.

6. What other type of text is related to this story?

(A) a poem about space

(B) a nonfiction text about a space shuttle

(C) a science–fiction novel about living in space in the future

(D) a fictional story about Earth being polluted

1. (Y)(N)

2. (Y)(N)

3. (Y)(N)

4. (Y)(N)

5. (Y)(N)

6. (Y)(N)

___ / 6

Total

SCORE

___ / 4

NAME:_____ **DATE:**_____

DIRECTIONS Reread "The War in Space." Then, read the prompt and respond on the lines below.

Think about what life would be like to live in space. What would you miss most about living on Earth, and why?

_____

_____

_____

_____

_____

_____

_____

_____

_____

_____

_____

_____

_____

_____

_____

_____

_____

NAME:_____ DATE:_____

DIRECTIONS   Read the text and then answer the questions.

Is soccer the same as football, or are they two different sports? Well, it depends on whom you ask. Americans know soccer as a kicking game played with goals. Football involves tackling. Touchdowns are scored instead of goals. Other countries have different names for these games. Some call the kicking game football instead of soccer. It can be very confusing!

1. Which chapter title would help a reader who is previewing this text?

- (A) Kicking the Ball
- (B) Soccer or Football?
- (C) American Sports
- (D) Tackling Sport

2. Which index entry would point a reader to this text?

- (A) soccer rules
- (B) names of games
- (C) sports heroes
- (D) football injuries

3. Which word has the same vowel sound as *games*?

- (A) gander
- (B) gash
- (C) time
- (D) aim

4. What is the antonym of the word *confusing*?

- (A) quick
- (B) dark
- (C) obvious
- (D) difficult

5. What does the phrase *it depends on whom you ask* mean in the text?

- (A) Some people will not know the answer.
- (B) Some people will be rude if you ask them.
- (C) You will get different answers from different people.
- (D) People agree on the answer.

1. (Y)(N)

2. (Y)(N)

3. (Y)(N)

4. (Y)(N)

5. (Y)(N)

___ / 5
Total

NAME: _____ **DATE:** _____

SCORE

1. Ⓨ Ⓝ

2. Ⓨ Ⓝ

3. Ⓨ Ⓝ

4. Ⓨ Ⓝ

5. Ⓨ Ⓝ

___ / 5
Total

DIRECTIONS Read the text and then answer the questions.

The offside rule in soccer is good to know. A player can be called offside. This happens when a player stands closer to an opponent's goal than the ball and a defending player. A player cannot receive a pass by the goal and the goalie. This rule makes the soccer game fair. It keeps players from hanging out by the goal and waiting for a pass.

1. Which statement summarizes the text?

Ⓐ This text explains how referees make calls about rules.

Ⓑ This text explains how kids learn soccer skills.

Ⓒ This text explains what rules are easily broken during a soccer game.

Ⓓ This text explains what the offside rule is.

2. Which chapter title best fits this text?

Ⓐ Scoring a Goal

Ⓑ Soccer Fans

Ⓒ Soccer Rules

Ⓓ Breaking the Rules

3. Which two words have the same vowel sound?

Ⓐ *good* and *know*

Ⓑ *not* and *goal*

Ⓒ *keeps* and *receives*

Ⓓ *ball* and *pass*

4. What is the antonym of *opponent*?

Ⓐ friend

Ⓑ teammate

Ⓒ coach

Ⓓ teacher

5. What does the phrase *makes the soccer game fair* mean in the text?

Ⓐ slowing people down

Ⓑ prevents people from cheating

Ⓒ makes the game fun to watch

Ⓓ keeps coaches happy

NAME:_____ **DATE:**_____

| DIRECTIONS | Read the text and then answer the questions. |

Where can a fan watch the best male soccer players in the world? At the World Cup, of course. The World Cup is the biggest soccer competition in the world. It happens every four years. There are 32 teams that compete for the winning title. Brazil has won the most titles, winning five times.

1. Which sentence gives the main idea?

Ⓐ the first sentence

Ⓑ the second sentence

Ⓒ the third sentence

Ⓓ the last sentence

2. Which title best fits this text?

Ⓐ The Ultimate Champion

Ⓑ Playing to Win

Ⓒ The World Cup

Ⓓ Game Tickets

3. Which two words have the same root word?

Ⓐ *compete* and *competition*

Ⓑ *male* and *most*

Ⓒ *team* and *title*

Ⓓ *compete* and *course*

4. What is an antonym of *competition*?

Ⓐ win

Ⓑ cooperation

Ⓒ game

Ⓓ battle

5. The sentence *At the World Cup, of course* shows that the author

Ⓐ dislikes the World Cup.

Ⓑ thinks most readers know about the World Cup.

Ⓒ is going to the World Cup.

Ⓓ is a soccer player on a World Cup team.

1. Ⓨ Ⓝ

2. Ⓨ Ⓝ

3. Ⓨ Ⓝ

4. Ⓨ Ⓝ

5. Ⓨ Ⓝ

___ / 5
Total

NAME: _____ DATE: _____

Kicking It with Beckham

Many young boys and girls grow up wanting to become a famous athlete. David Beckham did. Many people that know him say that he was born to be a soccer player. He has loved the game from a very young age.

David grew up in England. He lived a pretty simple life. He played soccer constantly as a young boy. He worked hard on his skills. It has always been the biggest part of his life. He played his first professional game as a young man. He was only 18 years old. He played for the Manchester United team.

Beckham quickly became a fan favorite. He plays midfield and helps to move the ball for his team. He got a lot of attention for one goal he made. During a game, he noticed a goalie who was out of the goal. He kicked a goal from the halfway line of the field. He made it! Many people started to notice David after this play. He continued to work hard. Beckham helped his team win many games. He was also in the running for the World Player of the Year. People enjoyed watching him play.

In 2003, he was transferred to the Real Madrid team in Spain. He began to earn a lot of money for his smart footwork! His life truly became a rags-to-riches story. Beckham came from a simple life to earn millions of dollars playing soccer.

David Beckham

Today, David Beckham plays with the Los Angeles Galaxy team. He has dealt with several injuries in his career. Because of them, he has missed some games. Yet David Beckham remains one of the great soccer players in the world.

NAME: _____ **DATE:** _____

DIRECTIONS Read "Kicking It with Beckham" and then answer the questions.

1. Which question shows a purpose for reading this text?

Ⓐ How much is a professional athlete paid?

Ⓑ How did David Beckham become a great soccer player?

Ⓒ Which soccer team has won the most championships?

Ⓓ What are the rules for soccer?

2. Which sentence shares the author's opinion?

Ⓐ People enjoyed watching him play.

Ⓑ Beckham quickly became a fan favorite.

Ⓒ Yet David Beckham remains one of the great soccer players in the world.

Ⓓ He has loved the game from a very young age.

3. Which statement shows a connection to this text?

Ⓐ This reminds me of being a fan of a movie star.

Ⓑ This reminds me of reading a story like "Hansel and Gretel."

Ⓒ This reminds me of playing at the beach.

Ⓓ This reminds me of working hard to learn how to play tennis.

4. Which event happened first?

Ⓐ Beckham joined the Los Angeles Galaxy team.

Ⓑ Beckham scored a goal from midfield.

Ⓒ Beckham missed games because of injuries.

Ⓓ Beckham played for the Manchester United team.

5. What is the most important point about Beckham's life?

Ⓐ He was only 18 when he became a professional soccer player.

Ⓑ He worked hard, and his life story went from rags to riches.

Ⓒ He played for three different teams.

Ⓓ He grew up in England.

6. How many professional soccer teams are mentioned?

Ⓐ one team

Ⓑ two teams

Ⓒ three teams

Ⓓ four teams

1. Ⓨ Ⓝ

2. Ⓨ Ⓝ

3. Ⓨ Ⓝ

4. Ⓨ Ⓝ

5. Ⓨ Ⓝ

6. Ⓨ Ⓝ

___ / 6
Total

NAME:_____ **DATE:**_____

SCORE

___ / 4

DIRECTIONS Reread "Kicking It with Beckham." Then, read the prompt and respond on the lines below.

Think about how David Beckham worked hard to become very good at his sport. Describe something that you work hard at and practice. What motivates you to keep practicing?

_____

_____

_____

_____

_____

_____

_____

_____

_____

_____

_____

_____

_____

_____

_____

NAME:_____ DATE:_____

DIRECTIONS Read the text and then answer the questions.

The bank clerk counted money each day. He helped customers who waited in line. He had to use all different forms of cash and coins. Some people had checks they needed to deposit. Each customer was different. The clerk never knew what to expect. Working in a bank was like a juggling act.

1. Ⓨ Ⓝ

2. Ⓨ Ⓝ

3. Ⓨ Ⓝ

1. What is this text about?

Ⓐ It is about someone who robs a bank.

Ⓑ It is about a clerk at an office.

Ⓒ It is about a bank clerk's job.

Ⓓ It is about banks around the world.

4. Ⓨ Ⓝ

3. Which two words from the text have the same vowel sound?

Ⓐ *line* and *need*

Ⓑ *what* and *was*

Ⓒ *bank* and *act*

Ⓓ *each* and *coin*

5. Ⓨ Ⓝ

2. What did the bank clerk do at his job?

Ⓐ counted money

Ⓑ helped customers in line

Ⓒ used different forms of cash and coins

Ⓓ all of the above

____ / 5

Total

4. What word has the same root word as *needed*?

Ⓐ needle

Ⓑ needs

Ⓒ knee

Ⓓ Ned

5. What is the simile in this text?

Ⓐ counted money each day

Ⓑ never knew what to expect

Ⓒ each customer was different

Ⓓ working in a bank was like a juggling act

NAME: _____ DATE: _____

DIRECTIONS Read the text and then answer the questions.

1. Ⓨ Ⓝ

2. Ⓨ Ⓝ

3. Ⓨ Ⓝ

Sam's mom pulled out her credit card to pay for the groceries. "Mom, why do you use a card to pay for things?" Sam asked. His mom explained how a credit card works. She still pays money for their food, but she just puts charges on her credit card. Then, she pays the credit card bill at the end of the month. This helps her stay on a budget. It also means she does not have to carry money around. Now Sam understands that everything is bought with money, even if you use a credit card at a store.

4. Ⓨ Ⓝ

5. Ⓨ Ⓝ

1. Which title would tell a reader more about this text?

Ⓐ Sam's Discussion
Ⓑ A Lesson About Credit Cards
Ⓒ Budgeting Cash
Ⓓ A Trip to the Store

___ / 5
Total

2. What is the setting of the text?

Ⓐ a bank
Ⓑ an airport
Ⓒ a dinner table
Ⓓ a grocery store

3. Which word in the text has the same first sound as the word *change*?

Ⓐ carry
Ⓑ charges
Ⓒ card
Ⓓ credit

4. What is a synonym for *budget*?

Ⓐ charge
Ⓑ money plan
Ⓒ quarter
Ⓓ coin

5. *Then* and *Now* are words that tell the reader

Ⓐ the importance of information presented in the text.
Ⓑ the order of events.
Ⓒ to reread the sentence.
Ⓓ the solution to the problem.

NAME:_____ **DATE:**_____

DIRECTIONS Read the text and then answer the questions.

> Sammy and Justin had been inside all day. It was pouring rain outside. Soccer games were cancelled. The two brothers were bored. "Make something interesting," their mom told them. The boys thought about it. They decided to build a fort. It was so much fun to play inside! Then, the fort started to collapse. There were pillows and blankets everywhere. "Let's clean up. We can work together," their mom said. "Teamwork helps everyone carry a lighter load."

1. Ⓨ Ⓝ

2. Ⓨ Ⓝ

3. Ⓨ Ⓝ

1. Which picture would tell a reader more about this text?

Ⓐ a picture of a blanket fort

Ⓑ a picture of a soccer ball

Ⓒ a picture of a pillow

Ⓓ a picture of two brothers

4. Ⓨ Ⓝ

5. Ⓨ Ⓝ

4. Which of these words mean the same thing?

Ⓐ *bored* and *interesting*

Ⓑ *load* and *fort*

Ⓒ *inside* and *outside*

Ⓓ *work together* and *teamwork*

___ / 5
Total

2. Which title best fits the main idea of this text?

Ⓐ Pillows and Blankets

Ⓑ Rainy Day Fun

Ⓒ Brothers

Ⓓ Clean-Up

5. A *lighter load* is an example of

Ⓐ tone.

Ⓑ a metaphor.

Ⓒ a theme.

Ⓓ a simile.

3. Which word is the root word in *decided*?

Ⓐ cide

Ⓑ decide

Ⓒ ded

Ⓓ cided

NAME: _____ DATE: _____

Money in the Bank

I have been doing chores around my house since I was very little. I like to help my parents. I also like to get an allowance. My dad gives me some money each month after my chores are done.

Part of me wants to run out and spend my money right away. I always have my eye on some kind of toy or gadget. But I don't just spend my money. My dad helps me to divide my money equally. My money goes into three categories: I put some money in my savings, I set some money aside for donating, and I keep some money for spending. This way I can spend, save, and donate all at the same time. I have watched my savings grow over the years. I have new ideas all the time about how to spend my savings. For now, it stays in the bank.

The donated money goes to different places. This is where I can help people who need it. One place I really like to help is the Nature Preserve. I love animals of all kinds. The Nature Preserve takes care of injured wild animals. They need donations to help buy food and supplies for the animals. They even send me a thank-you card after I make a donation.

I think my parents are teaching me good lessons about money. I have learned how to say no to myself! I often see things I want to buy. Sometimes my friends will get new toys, and I want something, too. But I always think about how much something costs. I wonder if it is worth it. Should I dip into my savings? Do I have enough to spend? These are good ways to practice being responsible with money.

NAME:_____ DATE:_____

DIRECTIONS Read "Money in the Bank" and then answer the questions.

SCORE

1. What is the text about?

(A) This is about having no money in the bank.

(B) This is about spending and saving money wisely.

(C) This is about touring a bank.

(D) This is about stealing.

2. What is the author's opinion?

(A) An allowance is not important for most kids.

(B) It is important to save and donate money, too.

(C) The Nature Preserve needs donations.

(D) A parent is in charge of a child's money.

3. Who would best relate to the narrator's experience?

(A) someone who donates old clothes to people in need

(B) a child who is learning about coins and bills

(C) someone trying to save money for a new house

(D) a visitor to the Nature Preserve

4. Which statement is true about the narrator?

(A) She spends too much money on silly things.

(B) She wants to spend all the money right away but does not.

(C) She likes to donate money to her school.

(D) She does not understand how to save money.

5. What is a theme of this text?

(A) Learning about money is important at any age.

(B) Saving a little bit of money is not worth it.

(C) Dividing your money is very difficult.

(D) Donations should only go to places that help animals.

6. What other type of text is similar to this text?

(A) a letter asking for a donation

(B) a nonfiction text about being smart with money

(C) a story about a child who loses money on a school field trip

(D) a nonfiction text about printing new dollar bills

1. (Y)(N)

2. (Y)(N)

3. (Y)(N)

4. (Y)(N)

5. (Y)(N)

6. (Y)(N)

___ / 6

Total

NAME: _____ **DATE:** _____

DIRECTIONS Reread "Money in the Bank." Then, read the prompt and respond on the lines below.

Think about how the narrator divides up her allowance. Does this system make sense to you? Why or why not?

_____

_____

_____

_____

_____

_____

_____

_____

_____

_____

_____

_____

_____

_____

_____

_____

NAME: _____ **DATE:** _____

DIRECTIONS Read the text and then answer the questions.

Female athletes have not always been respected. Some sports only allow men to play. Many people ignore female sports. The Olympics used to do this, too. At first, no women were allowed to play in the Olympic Games. This changed in 1900. This was when women were allowed to compete. Today, female athletes win a lot of medals! Women's sports are a lot of fun to watch in the Games.

1. Ⓨ Ⓝ

2. Ⓨ Ⓝ

3. Ⓨ Ⓝ

4. Ⓨ Ⓝ

5. Ⓨ Ⓝ

___ / 5

Total

1. Which question about the text would help readers monitor their reading?

Ⓐ When were women allowed to play in the Olympics?

Ⓑ What sport should I play at recess?

Ⓒ Who is respected at our school?

Ⓓ What happened in 1920?

2. Which title best fits the text?

Ⓐ The Events of 1900

Ⓑ Women in Sports

Ⓒ Olympic Games

Ⓓ Changes to Come

3. Which word has the same vowel sound as *play*?

Ⓐ plaid

Ⓑ wave

Ⓒ plan

Ⓓ sandy

4. What is a synonym for *allow*?

Ⓐ count

Ⓑ loud

Ⓒ let

Ⓓ hear

5. Which word describes the tone of the this text?

Ⓐ factual

Ⓑ funny

Ⓒ personal

Ⓓ persuasive

NAME: _____ DATE: _____

DIRECTIONS Read the text and then answer the questions.

SCORE

1. Y N

2. Y N

3. Y N

4. Y N

5. Y N

___ / 5
Total

Many fans enjoy watching Olympic events. Some people have a favorite sport. They watch the athletes and root for them. They hope that a favorite athlete will win a medal. It is fun to watch people who are in great shape. The athletes work hard for the Olympic Games. They train for years. The Olympic Games help people's dreams come true.

1. What is the main focus of this text?

Ⓐ dreams

Ⓑ Olympic events

Ⓒ medals

Ⓓ hard work

2. Which title best fits the text?

Ⓐ Rooting for the Team

Ⓑ Olympic Athletes and Events

Ⓒ Getting in Shape

Ⓓ Too Much Hard Work

3. Which two words from the text have the same vowel sound?

Ⓐ *win* and *their*

Ⓑ *games* and *fans*

Ⓒ *true* and *root*

Ⓓ *hope* and *come*

4. Which word is a synonym for *root* as it is used in this text?

Ⓐ source

Ⓑ plant

Ⓒ search

Ⓓ cheer

5. What other type of text is most similar to this text?

Ⓐ a math book

Ⓑ a story about frogs

Ⓒ a menu

Ⓓ an article about training for sports

NAME:_____ DATE:_____

DIRECTIONS Read the text and then answer the questions.

   The Olympic Games have a special symbol. It is five rings that are connected. The rings are blue, yellow, black, green, and red. They are shown on a white background. These five rings represent the idea that all countries are welcome to join the Games. The colors were chosen to include the colors of every nation's flag. This symbol is shown on flags that are flown at the Olympic Games.

1. Ⓨ Ⓝ

2. Ⓨ Ⓝ

3. Ⓨ Ⓝ

1. Which type of image would tell a reader more about this text?

Ⓐ a picture of a blank flag
Ⓑ a time line showing 1912
Ⓒ a picture of the Olympic symbol
Ⓓ a photograph of an athlete

4. Which of these words has the same root word as *designed*?

Ⓐ designer
Ⓑ sing
Ⓒ describe
Ⓓ danger

4. Ⓨ Ⓝ

5. Ⓨ Ⓝ

2. Which title best fits the text?

Ⓐ Many Colors
Ⓑ Flag Colors
Ⓒ The Big Games
Ⓓ The Symbol of the Olympics

5. What is true about the Olympic symbol?

Ⓐ The symbol's design includes countries from around the world.
Ⓑ The symbol needs to be redesigned.
Ⓒ The symbol represents only a few countries.
Ⓓ The symbol is rarely seen.

___ / 5
Total

3. What do context clues tell you about the meaning of the word *connected*?

Ⓐ related
Ⓑ linked
Ⓒ colored
Ⓓ big

NAME: _____ DATE: _____

The History of the Olympics

The Olympic Torch in Beijing, 2008

The Olympics are games played every two years. Countries from around the world compete. Athletes win medals. Gold is for first place. Silver is for second place. Bronze is for third place. The Games move from place to place. It is an honor for any city to host the Olympic Games. They are a tradition that people from all over enjoy watching.

The Olympics are divided into Winter Games and Summer Games. They alternate, so every two years, one of the games is played. The Winter Games host winter sports. These include skating and skiing. They also include the bobsled and luge. There are 15 winter sports.

The Summer Games host summer sports. Swimming is a popular summer sport. So are cycling and track events. There are 42 summer sports.

There have been a few rare times when there were no Olympics. World War I and World War II forced people to cancel the Games. This happened in 1916, 1940, and 1944.

The Olympic Games have been around for thousands of years. They began in Greece. They started in ancient times. Ancient Greeks liked competitions. They took the Games seriously.

Over the years, sports that are played in the Games have changed. In fact, the first Games had only one sport. It was called the *stade*. It was a foot race. Today's sports change every once in a while. There used to be a boating competition. Polo was also played at the games. These two sports are no longer part of the Olympics.

The Olympics are a part of history. They are a symbol of goodwill. They bring people together from all over the world. People are happy to see who will win or lose. Yet the Olympics are about more than winning. They are about being a part of a tradition. They are about celebrating the global community.

 #50924—180 Days of Reading for Third Grade

NAME:_____ DATE:_____

DIRECTIONS Read "The History of the Olympics" and then answer the questions.

1. What is a reasonable prediction based on the title?

Ⓐ This is a fictional story about attending the modern Games.

Ⓑ This is a nonfiction text about the history of the Olympics.

Ⓒ This is a text about the history of a family named the Olympics.

Ⓓ This is a nonfiction text about a town named Olympics.

2. What is the author's purpose?

Ⓐ to describe who won the most gold medals

Ⓑ to persuade others to buy tickets to the Games

Ⓒ to teach about the history of the Olympic Games

Ⓓ to teach about World War I

3. Which statement makes a connection to the text?

Ⓐ I like playing in soccer tournaments.

Ⓑ I watched some of the 2012 London Olympics events.

Ⓒ I won first place in a chess tournament.

Ⓓ I don't enjoy watching sports.

4. The sixth paragraph would work best in a text about

Ⓐ changes in Olympic events.

Ⓑ the Olympics in 2008.

Ⓒ life in ancient Greece.

Ⓓ the Olympic medals.

5. What is the main idea?

Ⓐ The Olympics are special games that bring people around the world together.

Ⓑ The Winter Games include skiing.

Ⓒ The Summer Games include swimming.

Ⓓ The Olympics are played every four years.

6. Why are people from around the world involved with the Olympics?

Ⓐ because it is on television everywhere

Ⓑ because athletes from all countries can compete

Ⓒ because the winners become very rich

Ⓓ because everyone wants to be an Olympic athlete

1. Ⓨ Ⓝ

2. Ⓨ Ⓝ

3. Ⓨ Ⓝ

4. Ⓨ Ⓝ

5. Ⓨ Ⓝ

6. Ⓨ Ⓝ

___ / 6
Total

NAME: _____ **DATE:** _____

DIRECTIONS Reread "The History of the Olympics." Then, read the prompt and respond on the lines below.

The author shared many facts about the Olympic Games. Which facts were the most interesting to you? Why?

_____

_____

_____

_____

_____

_____

_____

_____

_____

_____

_____

_____

_____

_____

_____

NAME: _____ **DATE:** _____

DIRECTIONS Read the text and then answer the questions.

"Peter, did you walk Lucy today?" his mom asked. Peter was in charge of taking his dog for a walk. Lucy needed a walk every day. Even if it was a short walk, she needed her exercise. Peter had agreed to take care of Lucy when he asked for a puppy. He knew that pets were a lot of work. He did not care. Peter loved Lucy like a best friend.

1. Ⓨ Ⓝ

2. Ⓨ Ⓝ

3. Ⓨ Ⓝ

1. What is this text about?

Ⓐ exercising

Ⓑ a boy and his dog

Ⓒ pets

Ⓓ friends

2. Who is the main character?

Ⓐ Lucy

Ⓑ Peter's mom

Ⓒ Lucy's mom

Ⓓ Peter

3. What word part could you add to the root *ask* to make a new word?

Ⓐ –es

Ⓑ –ly

Ⓒ –ing

Ⓓ –ful

4. What is the definition of *exercise*?

Ⓐ companionship

Ⓑ a physical workout

Ⓒ food

Ⓓ fetch

5. Which phrase is a simile from this text?

Ⓐ *in charge of*

Ⓑ *agreed to take care of*

Ⓒ *like a best friend*

Ⓓ *a lot of work*

4. Ⓨ Ⓝ

5. Ⓨ Ⓝ

___ / 5

Total

NAME:_____ DATE:_____

DIRECTIONS Read the text and then answer the questions.

1. Ⓨ Ⓝ

2. Ⓨ Ⓝ

3. Ⓨ Ⓝ

4. Ⓨ Ⓝ

5. Ⓨ Ⓝ

___/ 5
Total

A talking parrot can be a very funny pet. Sometimes it may even scare you a bit. One night, I came home with my parents, and the living room was dark. Before we could turn on a light, we heard a voice call out our names. We were so scared because we thought there was a burglar in our house. It turned out to be our parrot greeting us. We laughed for a long time after that happened.

1. Which title would tell a reader more about this text?

Ⓐ Pirates and Their Birds

Ⓑ Scared by a Parrot

Ⓒ Is That a Burglar?

Ⓓ A Funny Story

2. Who is the narrator?

Ⓐ a child

Ⓑ a mother

Ⓒ a father

Ⓓ a parrot

3. Which word has the same vowel sound as *scare*?

Ⓐ score

Ⓑ spare

Ⓒ cane

Ⓓ rack

4. Which word is a synonym for *greeting*?

Ⓐ pecking

Ⓑ yelling

Ⓒ welcoming

Ⓓ talking

5. Which word describes the tone of this text?

Ⓐ informative

Ⓑ serious

Ⓒ funny

Ⓓ false

NAME:_____ **DATE:**_____

DIRECTIONS Read the text and then answer the questions.

Wade could barely sit still at school. All he could think about was what was going on at his house right now. Wade's mind was on his sweet dog, Mabel. Mabel was due to have puppies any minute. Wade's family had homes for all the babies already. The new owners were just waiting. Wade wondered if Mabel would deliver today. He thought about his pet the entire way home on the bus.

1. Ⓨ Ⓝ

2. Ⓨ Ⓝ

3. Ⓨ Ⓝ

1. Which picture would tell a reader more about this text?

Ⓐ a picture of a dog with puppies

Ⓑ a picture of a clock

Ⓒ a picture of a schoolhouse

Ⓓ a picture of a school bus

4. Which of these words are synonyms?

Ⓐ *barely* and *think*

Ⓑ *wondered* and *thought*

Ⓒ *sit* and *still*

Ⓓ *minute* and *today*

4. Ⓨ Ⓝ

5. Ⓨ Ⓝ

2. Which title best fits this text?

Ⓐ Mabel's Secret

Ⓑ Waiting for Puppies

Ⓒ Getting Ready

Ⓓ Hard to Wait

5. Which is an example of alliteration from the text?

Ⓐ sit still at school

Ⓑ his house

Ⓒ Wade wondered

Ⓓ all of the above

____ / 5

Total

3. Which word is the root word in *going*?

Ⓐ ing

Ⓑ go

Ⓒ oing

Ⓓ goin

NAME: _____ DATE: _____

The Cutest Face in the World

The Ling family did not think they were going home with a pet that day. Annie wanted to visit the animal shelter. She wanted to see the cats and dogs. She had wanted a pet for years. Her parents were waiting for the girls to be old enough. Annie was seven. Her sister Lily was only three. Lily was still learning how to act around animals. She had a lot of energy!

Annie and Lily were excited to see the animals. A shelter volunteer gave the Ling family a tour. The volunteer talked about why animals came to the shelter. Some were found by the road. Others were dropped off by families who could not care for them.

Finally, the Ling family got to see the animals. There was a cat section and a dog section. They were all so cute! Some of the animals looked scared. This made Annie sad. The volunteer explained that animals need time to get used to a new place. She assured Annie that all the people caring for these animals were kind.

The Ling family walked through the dog section. They started talking. A dog just felt like the right choice. Annie's mom could not take her eyes off an older black dog with kind eyes. Annie's dad was interested in a large, energetic dog. Annie had found her own favorite. He was a young puppy. He was brown with spots. He had been found near the railroad track with six other puppies. Annie could not take her eyes off this dog. She thought he had the cutest face in the world.

Annie pleaded with her parents. They did not want to make a quick decision. Pets are a big responsibility. But they could see in Annie's eyes that she had found her companion. The volunteer talked about what a good breed the dog was and that he would be kind with children. That was what the family needed to hear. They had made up their minds! This little one was coming home!

NAME: _____ **DATE:** _____

DIRECTIONS Read "The Cutest Face in the World" and then answer the questions.

1. Which statement summarizes the text?

Ⓐ Annie meets another child who has a cute face.

Ⓑ Annie has the cutest face in the world.

Ⓒ Annie meets her new dog, and he has the cutest face in the world.

Ⓓ Annie's family argues over who has the cutest face in the world.

2. The author would likely agree that

Ⓐ an animal shelter can be a good place to find a pet.

Ⓑ any pet can live with any family.

Ⓒ pets are easy to care for.

Ⓓ people should only adopt puppies.

3. Which statement shows a personal connection to the text?

Ⓐ My brother is allergic to dogs.

Ⓑ My family adopted our cat from a shelter.

Ⓒ Snakes make good pets.

Ⓓ I volunteer at my school.

4. What was the big change for the characters?

Ⓐ Annie and her mother finally agree on a pet.

Ⓑ The Ling family decided to volunteer at the shelter.

Ⓒ They wanted to wait to get a pet, but they met the right one on the tour.

Ⓓ They wanted a cat but chose a dog.

5. What message does this text share about adopting pets?

Ⓐ Finding the right pet for your family is important.

Ⓑ There are more cats up for adoption than dogs.

Ⓒ Adopting a pet is difficult.

Ⓓ Shelters do not have sweet animals for families.

6. Which title below indicates a similar text?

Ⓐ Falling in Love with a Stray Cat

Ⓑ Preparing for a Baby

Ⓒ Moving to a New House

Ⓓ Opening Presents

1. Ⓨ Ⓝ

2. Ⓨ Ⓝ

3. Ⓨ Ⓝ

4. Ⓨ Ⓝ

5. Ⓨ Ⓝ

6. Ⓨ Ⓝ

___ / 6

Total

SCORE

___ / 4

NAME: _____ DATE: _____

DIRECTIONS Reread "The Cutest Face in the World." Then, read the prompt and respond on the lines below.

Think about how happy Annie must feel when she sees her future dog for the first time. When have you felt happy when something in your life was about to change? How would you describe that feeling?

_____

_____

_____

_____

_____

_____

_____

_____

_____

_____

_____

_____

_____

_____

_____

_____

NAME:_____ **DATE:**_____

DIRECTIONS Read the text and then answer the questions.

Can you imagine a world with no chocolate chip cookies? This yummy sweet did not always exist. It was invented by Ruth Wakefield. It happened in 1930. She worked at an inn. She baked sweets for her guests. One night, she made a decision. She cut pieces of a chocolate bar. She added them to her cookie batter. She wanted to make a chocolate cookie. She thought it would melt together. She was surprised the chocolate stayed in chunks!

SCORE

1. Ⓨ Ⓝ

2. Ⓨ Ⓝ

3. Ⓨ Ⓝ

4. Ⓨ Ⓝ

5. Ⓨ Ⓝ

___ / 5
Total

1. Which question about the text would help readers monitor their reading?

Ⓐ What comes in chunks like chocolate?

Ⓑ What else can people mix together?

Ⓒ Who invented the chocolate chip cookie?

Ⓓ Where is an inn near my house?

2. Which title best fits the text?

Ⓐ Mixing It Up

Ⓑ The First Chocolate Chip Cookie

Ⓒ Ruth's Sweets

Ⓓ Sweets for the Guests

3. Which word has the same vowel sound as *chip*?

Ⓐ inn

Ⓑ creek

Ⓒ cheap

Ⓓ type

4. What is the definition of *chunks* as it is used in this text?

Ⓐ lumps

Ⓑ rocks

Ⓒ large pieces

Ⓓ hard parts

5. Which word describes the tone of this text?

Ⓐ factual

Ⓑ serious

Ⓒ funny

Ⓓ persuasive

NAME:_____ DATE:_____

SCORE

1. Y N

2. Y N

3. Y N

4. Y N

5. Y N

___/5
Total

DIRECTIONS Read the text and then answer the questions.

Do you like to eat food? You could earn money doing that for a job! A food taster is a real career that many adults pursue. It is not as easy a job as you would think. Food tasters have to think a lot about how things smell, taste, and feel in their mouths. They have to be able to describe all of these sensations. Companies hire them to check their products before they go on store shelves.

1. Which type of image would tell a reader more about this text?

- A a picture of food
- B a picture of a food taster at work
- C a list of ingredients in a recipe
- D a picture of a plate and fork

2. Which chapter title would help a reader find this information in a table of contents?

- A Yummy!
- B The Work of a Food Taster
- C Easy Work
- D A Full Stomach

3. Which word is the root word in *tasters*?

- A toast
- B taster
- C taste
- D ster

4. Which word is a synonym for *pursue*?

- A hunt
- B go after
- C trail
- D follow

5. Which other type of text is most similar to this text?

- A a math book
- B a book of information about jobs
- C a cookbook
- D a writing textbook

NAME:_____ DATE:_____

DIRECTIONS Read the text and then answer the questions.

    Everyone prefers certain foods. We all have likes. We all have dislikes. Some people always taste food in a different way. These people are *super tasters*. They have a very intense sense of taste. Super tasters are very sensitive to certain tastes. Bitter things taste even more bitter. Salty foods taste saltier. Sweet things may taste too sweet. Comparing food tastes sure is a mystery!

1. Ⓨ Ⓝ

2. Ⓨ Ⓝ

3. Ⓨ Ⓝ

1. What does the first sentence tell you about this text?

Ⓐ It is a text about food preferences.

Ⓑ It is a text about food allergies.

Ⓒ It is a text about eating healthy.

Ⓓ It is a text about food throughout history.

2. Which image would help a reader understand this information?

Ⓐ a picture of a fork

Ⓑ a picture of a salt shaker

Ⓒ a picture of a person tasting food

Ⓓ none of the above

3. Which word from the text makes a new word by adding the prefix *dis–*?

Ⓐ sweet

Ⓑ sure

Ⓒ taste

Ⓓ mystery

4. Ⓨ Ⓝ

5. Ⓨ Ⓝ

___ / 5

Total

4. Which word has the same root word as *comparing*?

Ⓐ paring

Ⓑ comparison

Ⓒ computer

Ⓓ pare

5. Which word describes the tone of this text?

Ⓐ factual

Ⓑ serious

Ⓒ funny

Ⓓ persuasive

NAME:_____ **DATE:**_____

The Invention of Gum

Some inventors spend time trying to get an invention just right. They work hard on samples. They compare these samples. They try to get the very best product. Inventors may talk to other people. They may even show off their work to get ideas from others. The process is long and detailed.

Other inventions happen almost by accident. Something surprising happens. This surprise causes a person to have a new idea about something. That is all it takes. Chewing gum was invented this way. It came about by accident.

People have been chewing substances for many years. Early people chewed birch bark tar. Others chewed a type of resin from a tree. Still others liked substances that came from plants or grasses.

What we call chewing gum was made by chance. People in Mexico liked to chew something called *chicle*. This was a sap from sapodilla trees. A general in the Mexican army wanted to use the chicle. He wanted to sell it as a cheaper alternative for rubber.

An American inventor became involved. His name was Thomas Adams. He could not get the chicle to work as a substitute for rubber. He used chicle to try to invent other things. One day he popped the chicle into his mouth. He chewed it. He liked it. He added a flavor to the chicle. This was the first use of chewing gum.

Today, gum is a very popular product in stores. It comes in many flavors. It comes in many sizes and shapes. Some gum has sugar. Some does not. All gum is delicious, that is for sure!

NAME: _____ DATE: _____

DIRECTIONS Read "The Invention of Gum" and then answer the questions.

1. What is the purpose for reading this text?

(A) to learn how to make gum

(B) to be persuaded to buy gum

(C) to learn about how gum was invented

(D) to learn about all inventions

2. Which advice would the author most likely offer to inventors?

(A) Work many years until you are ready to share an invention.

(B) Keep trying things because you never know when you will invent something.

(C) Do not share your inventions with anyone.

(D) Be safe while you practice your inventions.

3. Who would likely make a connection to this text?

(A) a teacher who is interested in different countries

(B) a child who loves to see what will happen in science experiments

(C) an adult who speaks Spanish

(D) an adult who was a general in the war

4. What is being compared in this text?

(A) inventions that take a long time to figure out and inventions that are accidents

(B) the invention of rubber and the invention of gum

(C) the general and Thomas Adams

(D) Mexico and America

5. What is the main idea?

(A) Inventions happen in all sorts of ways.

(B) Inventions take a lot of time.

(C) Inventions require a lot of hard work.

(D) Inventors are usually lucky.

6. How does this text describe the invention of gum?

(A) It was a longtime experiment.

(B) It was a scientific breakthrough.

(C) It was a happy accident.

(D) It was a mistake.

1. Y N

2. Y N

3. Y N

4. Y N

5. Y N

6. Y N

___ / 6
Total

NAME:_____ DATE:_____

SCORE

___ / 4

DIRECTIONS Reread "The Invention of Gum." Then, read the prompt and respond on the lines below.

Have you ever discovered something by accident? If so, what was it? If not, what do you hope you could invent or discover?

_____

_____

_____

_____

_____

_____

_____

_____

_____

_____

_____

_____

_____

_____

_____

NAME:_____ **DATE:**_____

DIRECTIONS Read the text and then answer the questions.

> June was always telling stories. She talked about her family. They went on a lot of adventures. Her family loved her stories. Sometimes she would exaggerate. "It didn't happen quite like that," her mom said. "Where do your stories come from?"
>
> "I have a wild imagination!" June would say.

1. Which title best fits this text?

- Ⓐ June's Family
- Ⓑ Exaggerated Stories
- Ⓒ Imaginations
- Ⓓ Storytelling

2. June has a conflict with

- Ⓐ her mother.
- Ⓑ herself.
- Ⓒ her teacher.
- Ⓓ her brother.

3. Which two words from the text have the same vowel sound?

- Ⓐ *her* and *went*
- Ⓑ *lot* and *loved*
- Ⓒ *come* and *from*
- Ⓓ *that* and *was*

4. Which word has the root word *happen*?

- Ⓐ happy
- Ⓑ hap
- Ⓒ happened
- Ⓓ open

5. What does the phrase *wild imagination* mean?

- Ⓐ pretending to be an animal
- Ⓑ thinking about wild animals
- Ⓒ having a good imagination and coming up with lots of ideas
- Ⓓ having little imagination

1. Ⓨ Ⓝ

2. Ⓨ Ⓝ

3. Ⓨ Ⓝ

4. Ⓨ Ⓝ

5. Ⓨ Ⓝ

___ / 5
Total

NAME:_____ DATE:_____

DIRECTIONS Read the text and then answer the questions.

The Strong Man in the circus was amazing to watch. He could lift very heavy things, sometimes with just one hand! The crowd was in awe of his strength. He would lift huge weights as though they were as light as a feather. People wondered how a person got to be so strong. The Strong Man was definitely one of the best acts of the show.

1. Which title would tell a reader more about this text?

Ⓐ A Circus

Ⓑ The Strong Man

Ⓒ Lifting Weights

Ⓓ Amazing Strength

2. What is the text about?

Ⓐ being as light as a feather

Ⓑ a crowd pleaser

Ⓒ the Strong Man's popular circus act

Ⓓ a crowded circus

3. Which word has the same vowel sound as *powder*?

Ⓐ show

Ⓑ awe

Ⓒ how

Ⓓ watch

4. What is a definition of the word *awe*?

Ⓐ fear

Ⓑ admiration

Ⓒ invisible

Ⓓ hurt

5. Which phrase from the text is a simile?

Ⓐ amazing to watch

Ⓑ as light as a feather

Ⓒ lift huge weights

Ⓓ one of the best acts

 #50924—180 Days of Reading for Third Grade

NAME:_____ DATE:_____

DIRECTIONS Read the text and then answer the questions.

The lumberjacks went to work on the tree. They knew that it had to come down today. They got all their tools ready to cut it. It was hard work that required a lot of strength and focus to keep safe. The lumberjacks were part of a team that relied on one another. It took many of them working together to bring some of those big trees down safely!

1. Ⓨ Ⓝ

2. Ⓨ Ⓝ

3. Ⓨ Ⓝ

1. Who are the main characters?

Ⓐ lumberjacks

Ⓑ trees

Ⓒ tools

Ⓓ strong people

2. What is the setting?

Ⓐ in a lumber mill

Ⓑ in a forest

Ⓒ in a large city

Ⓓ in a truck

3. Which two words have the same vowel sound?

Ⓐ cut and work

Ⓑ got and down

Ⓒ trees and tools

Ⓓ each and trees

4. Which word has the same root as relied?

Ⓐ really

Ⓑ reliable

Ⓒ elie

Ⓓ reel

5. Which title best fits the text?

Ⓐ Cut Down All the Trees

Ⓑ Working in the Forest

Ⓒ Lumberjack Larry

Ⓓ My Favorite Tools

4. Ⓨ Ⓝ

5. Ⓨ Ⓝ

___ / 5
Total

NAME: _____ DATE: _____

Paul Bunyan

Paul Bunyan was a big, tall, strong lumberjack. The story of his life is a folktale. It has been shared with each new generation. The story has been exaggerated. It is a folktale that many people still know.

Most tales of Paul Bunyan include his sidekick. A *sidekick* is a friend who is always by your side. Paul's sidekick was a blue ox called Babe. The stories of Paul and Babe all describe how strong Paul Bunyan was. In fact, when he was born, it took five storks to carry the infant! He was quite large. When he was just a week old, Paul had to wear his father's clothes.

As he grew older, Paul was always out with Babe and helping with different projects. Paul and Babe often used their strength to help people in need. One day, a group of loggers discovered a huge log jam. It was in the Wisconsin River. The logs were almost 200 feet high! The jam continued for a mile or more. Paul and Babe came to help. Babe got in the water and moved his tail back and forth. The water became quite rough, causing the jam to move upstream while moving the logs. With each movement of his tail, more logs began to break apart from the jam. Finally, the logs began to move more and float downstream.

The story of Paul Bunyan still lives on today. People enjoy hearing about the big, strong man and his big, strong ox.

NAME:_____ **DATE:**_____

DIRECTIONS Read "Paul Bunyan" and then answer the questions.

1. Which statement about Paul Bunyan is **not** correct?

(A) Paul Bunyan used his strength to help people.

(B) Paul Bunyan was larger than regular people.

(C) Paul Bunyan chopped down trees everywhere he went.

(D) Paul Bunyan had a companion who helped him.

2. Which sentence shows the author's opinion?

(A) Paul's sidekick was a blue ox called Babe.

(B) People enjoy hearing about the big, strong man and his big, strong ox.

(C) Paul and Babe came to help.

(D) Most tales of Paul Bunyan include his sidekick.

3. Who could make a personal connection to the text?

(A) a person who is very short and needs help reaching things

(B) a fisherman

(C) a person who has a large dog as a pet

(D) a lumberjack

4. Which word describes the Paul Bunyan character?

(A) awkward

(B) helpful

(C) clumsy

(D) serious

5. What does this text tell you about folktales?

(A) They are easily forgotten.

(B) They are about strong people.

(C) They are important stories passed down through the generations.

(D) They are shared at the holidays.

6. Which other story features a character who has an animal sidekick?

(A) *Sleeping Beauty*

(B) *The Three Little Bears*

(C) *Cinderella*

(D) *Curious George*

1. (Y) (N)

2. (Y) (N)

3. (Y) (N)

4. (Y) (N)

5. (Y) (N)

6. (Y) (N)

___ / 6
Total

NAME:_____ DATE:_____

DIRECTIONS Reread "Paul Bunyan." Then, read the prompt and respond on the lines below.

Think about an exaggerated story that you know or have heard. What is the story, and how do you know it has been exaggerated?

_____

_____

_____

_____

_____

_____

_____

_____

_____

_____

_____

_____

_____

_____

NAME:_____ DATE:_____

DIRECTIONS Read the text and then answer the questions.

Earth is always moving. We revolve around the sun once each year. This creates the four different seasons. We also rotate around Earth's axis every 24 hours. This is what causes night and day. Our night sky changes throughout the year. Our view of the constellations changes with each season.

1. Which title would tell a reader more about this text?

- Ⓐ Changes
- Ⓑ Earth's Movements
- Ⓒ The Sun and the Moon
- Ⓓ Earth

2. What is the main idea?

- Ⓐ Earth rotates around the sun in 24 hours.
- Ⓑ Earth revolves around the sun in one year.
- Ⓒ Earth revolves and rotates.
- Ⓓ The night sky changes.

3. Which two words have the same vowel sound?

- Ⓐ *year* and *with*
- Ⓑ *sky* and *night*
- Ⓒ *in* and *night*
- Ⓓ *our* and *for*

4. Which object would *rotate*?

- Ⓐ the wind
- Ⓑ a snake
- Ⓒ a wheel
- Ⓓ a kite

5. The language of the text suggests that the author is addressing

- Ⓐ Earth.
- Ⓑ the author.
- Ⓒ all humans.
- Ⓓ the sun.

SCORE

1. Ⓨ Ⓝ

2. Ⓨ Ⓝ

3. Ⓨ Ⓝ

4. Ⓨ Ⓝ

5. Ⓨ Ⓝ

___ / 5
Total

NAME:_____ DATE:_____

SCORE

DIRECTIONS Read the text and then answer the questions.

1. Ⓨ Ⓝ

2. Ⓨ Ⓝ

A *star chart* is a map of the night sky. It can also be called a *sky map*. It shows where stars and constellations are located in the sky. Like most maps, a star chart is labeled with the four directions. When a person observes the sky, it helps to hold the star chart in the correct direction. Then it is easy to compare what is on the map with what is in the sky.

3. Ⓨ Ⓝ

1. Which title best fits this text?

Ⓐ Four Directions

4. Ⓨ Ⓝ

Ⓑ Star Charts

Ⓒ Charts and Maps

5. Ⓨ Ⓝ

Ⓓ Using a Chart

2. Which best summarizes the main idea?

___ / 5

Total

Ⓐ Constellations tell stories.

Ⓑ The night sky is dark.

Ⓒ Star charts are maps of the night sky.

Ⓓ Map words are important.

3. Which words have the same vowel sound?

Ⓐ *like* and *is*

Ⓑ *use* and *four*

Ⓒ *star* and *chart*

Ⓓ *sky* and *point*

4. What object would most likely be *labeled*?

Ⓐ a plate

Ⓑ a package

Ⓒ a dog

Ⓓ a pencil

5. How are star charts and sky maps related?

Ⓐ They are two different names for the same item.

Ⓑ They must be used together to watch the night sky.

Ⓒ A star chart used to be called a *sky map*.

Ⓓ They are not related.

NAME:_____ DATE:_____

DIRECTIONS Read the text and then answer the questions.

Astronomy is a type of science. It looks at the universe. The universe is made up of many things. People who study the universe often pick one thing to investigate. They may focus on planets. They may study the stars. They may learn about the sun. This information helps us. People on Earth can learn about life in space.

1. ⓎⓃ

2. ⓎⓃ

3. ⓎⓃ

1. Which picture would tell a reader more about this text?

ⓐ a picture of an astronaut

ⓑ a picture of a microscope

ⓒ a picture of a scientist

ⓓ a picture of a planet

4. Which word does **not** mean the same as *investigate*?

ⓐ study

ⓑ explore

ⓒ examine

ⓓ ignore

4. ⓎⓃ

5. ⓎⓃ

2. What is the main idea?

ⓐ The sun and planets are part of the universe.

ⓑ Some people study stars.

ⓒ The science of astronomy teaches us about the universe.

ⓓ People on Earth like to think about space.

5. What other type of text is similar to this text?

ⓐ a science book

ⓑ a fantasy novel

ⓒ a picture of the planet Mars

ⓓ a journal or diary entry about a trip to the history museum

___ / 5
Total

3. Which word has the same root as *study*?

ⓐ tidy

ⓑ student

ⓒ suddenly

ⓓ stuff

NAME:_____ DATE:_____

The Night Sky

People say that the sky is dark at night. Yet there are also a lot of stars in the night sky. These stars twinkle and provide a lot of light. There is a lot to look at in the night sky!

The stars in the sky have guided people for centuries. Humans have always looked up to the sky. All humans have wondered about life beyond our planet. People have used the stars as a way to show direction.

Over time, stories have been told about the star patterns. These patterns are called *constellations*. There are eighty-eight official constellations. They divide the night sky. They change position slightly each season.

Many constellations are named from old Greek myths. The Greeks were one of the first cultures to create names for stars. They believed the star patterns were made by the gods. They named these patterns after animals and objects. They also named twelve patterns that make up the signs of the zodiac.

One star that is often used as a guide is called *Polaris*. Some stargazers call it the brightest star in the sky. Polaris is also known as the North Star. It never rises or sets. People easily find Polaris. They notice that it belongs to a well-known constellation. It is at the end of the handle of the Little Dipper. The Big Dipper and the Little Dipper are constellations that are easy to find.

One way that stargazers try to preserve the night sky is by fighting *light pollution*. This is not a type of pollution that most people consider. Yet it is very important to people who like to look at stars. Light pollution occurs when too many lights are on in an area. The lights may be from homes or cars. Businesses use a lot of light, too. Light makes it hard for people to see patterns in the dark sky.

NAME:_____ DATE:_____

DIRECTIONS Read "The Night Sky" and then answer the questions.

1. Which summary of this text is the most accurate?

(A) This is about someone hoping for a falling star.

(B) This is about finding constellations in the night sky.

(C) This is about living away from the city where you can see the stars clearly.

(D) This is about how the Big Dipper got its name.

2. What is the author's purpose?

(A) to describe each constellation

(B) to inform readers about the night sky

(C) to share Greek mythology

(D) to compare the night sky and the day sky

3. Which statement shows a personal connection to the text?

(A) The Big Dipper is the name of my favorite restaurant.

(B) I have read some myths before.

(C) My dad and I have used a star chart to look at constellations.

(D) I don't like darkness.

4. Which two topics are described in the same paragraph?

(A) using stars for guidance and writing stories about the zodiac

(B) the North Star and Greek mythology

(C) Polaris and light pollution

(D) The Big Dipper and the Little Dipper

5. What is the main idea?

(A) The night sky is filled with pictures created by stars.

(B) There are eighty-eight constellations.

(C) The zodiac is in the stars.

(D) Constellations are only visible by using a telescope.

6. Why is light pollution a problem?

(A) Light pollution happens when lights shine on air pollution.

(B) It must be pitch black in order to see any stars.

(C) It is hard to see constellations when there are too many lights.

(D) People who watch stars often leave garbage on the ground.

1. Ⓨ Ⓝ

2. Ⓨ Ⓝ

3. Ⓨ Ⓝ

4. Ⓨ Ⓝ

5. Ⓨ Ⓝ

6. Ⓨ Ⓝ

___ / 6
Total

NAME:_____ DATE:_____

SCORE

___ / 4

DIRECTIONS Reread "The Night Sky." Then, read the prompt and respond on the lines below.

Think about what you know about the night sky or have seen yourself. What personal connections can you make with this text?

_____

_____

_____

_____

_____

_____

_____

_____

_____

_____

_____

_____

_____

_____

_____

NAME:_____ DATE:_____

DIRECTIONS Read the text and then answer the questions.

It was a very late Sunday night. Things were winding down at the Lewis house. The family had just finished a long dinner with their relatives. Everyone was tired and ready for bed. Marcus and Violet were in their pajamas. They were heading to their rooms. "Not so fast!" their mother called out. "You are forgetting something. It is very important."

Marcus shouted, "We need to brush our teeth!"

1. Ⓨ Ⓝ

2. Ⓨ Ⓝ

3. Ⓨ Ⓝ

1. Which image would tell a reader more about this text?

Ⓐ a clock showing 9:00

Ⓑ a menu

Ⓒ a time line

Ⓓ a picture of a family getting ready for bed

4. Ⓨ Ⓝ

5. Ⓨ Ⓝ

3. What word has the same vowel sound as *rooms*?

Ⓐ hook

Ⓑ rub

Ⓒ tune

Ⓓ rod

___ / 5

Total

2. Which word describes the main characters at the end of the text?

Ⓐ forgetful

Ⓑ late

Ⓒ sad

Ⓓ angry

4. What is the definition of *relatives*?

Ⓐ friends

Ⓑ family members

Ⓒ neighbors

Ⓓ students

5. Which phrase means *ending*?

Ⓐ Not so fast!

Ⓑ very late

Ⓒ heading to

Ⓓ winding down

NAME: _____ DATE: _____

DIRECTIONS Read the text and then answer the questions.

"Why do I keep getting these headaches?" Dante wondered. So he asked his mom, and she decided they needed to see a doctor. After a few tests, they had an answer.

"I think you need glasses," the doctor said. Dante was upset because he did not want to wear glasses. He just knew that everyone would tease him, including his friends. This was the worst day of his life.

1. Which title best fits this text?

- Ⓐ A Terrible Headache
- Ⓑ Getting Glasses
- Ⓒ Dante and His Mom
- Ⓓ Mean Friends

2. What is one setting?

- Ⓐ the doctor's office
- Ⓑ the school nurse's office
- Ⓒ Dante's mom's car
- Ⓓ the school bus

3. Which word has the same vowel sound as *need*?

- Ⓐ near
- Ⓑ net
- Ⓒ wet
- Ⓓ ten

4. Which word is a synonym for *tease*?

- Ⓐ keep
- Ⓑ love
- Ⓒ bother
- Ⓓ talk

5. Which word describes the tone of this text?

- Ⓐ informative
- Ⓑ sad
- Ⓒ funny
- Ⓓ false

NAME: _____ **DATE:** _____

DIRECTIONS Read the text and then answer the questions.

A mother and her daughter went to an appointment. It was a checkup at the dentist's office. The dentist would clean and examine her teeth and take some X-rays. The patient was terrified and did not want to go. "I really, really hate going to the dentist," she said.

"I know, Mom," the young girl replied. "I don't really like the dentist either, but it will all be over soon."

1. (Y)(N)

2. (Y)(N)

3. (Y)(N)

4. (Y)(N)

5. (Y)(N)

1. What is this text about?

(A) It is about a girl who has a playdate with a friend.

(B) It is about a dentist who is mean and scary.

(C) It is about a mother and daughter who go to an appointment.

(D) It is about a class that goes on a field trip to the dentist.

2. Which title best describes the main idea of this text?

(A) An Appointment

(B) At the Dentist

(C) Helping a Scared Mom

(D) Exam and X-Ray

3. Which word could have a *sh–* blend added to it to make a new word?

(A) all

(B) said

(C) went

(D) an

4. Which is an antonym for *terrified*?

(A) hilarious

(B) cold

(C) angry

(D) fearless

5. When do you learn that the mom is the patient?

(A) the first sentence

(B) the first paragraph

(C) the last paragraph

(D) none of the above

___ / 5

Total

NAME: _____ DATE: _____

A New Kind of Smile

It was a day that Claire had been expecting for a while now. She knew she had to get braces put on her teeth. Her dentist had broken the news at her last appointment. Several of her teeth were not growing in straight, which might cause problems with her other teeth as she grew older. The best solution was to have braces. They would be on her teeth for about two years.

At the time, Claire had been very sad to think about having braces for two years. She thought of all the food she would not be able to eat. She thought of how she would have a new and different smile. She was not happy about this change. She did not want to have something that made her stand out in the crowd.

Claire was also worried that braces would hurt. Her dentist said they would feel just fine. They might take a bit to get used to, but they would not hurt. That had made Claire feel better, but she was still nervous.

The big day finally came, and Claire made her way to the orthodontist's office. Claire sat still through the entire procedure. She watched a show on the television above her head. She tried to think of something else so that she did not get scared. It seemed to take forever for the orthodontist to finish, but finally, he told her to sit up and take a look at the mirror.

Claire was surprised at first. Her smile was new, and there was all this metal to look at now! She did not know how she would be able to wait two years for these things to come off, but there was no other option. Claire's mom took her to get ice cream to cheer her up. She just had to get used to the change. It would all be worth it because she would have a beautiful smile to enjoy for years to come!

NAME:_____ DATE:_____

DIRECTIONS Read "A New Kind of Smile" and then answer the questions.

1. Which prediction based on the title and image is the most accurate?

(A) It is about a child who has no teeth.

(B) It is about a person who does not know how to smile.

(C) It is about a child who needs braces.

(D) It is about a person who has never lost a tooth.

2. The author would most likely agree that

(A) braces make you popular.

(B) braces are temporary and are worth wearing.

(C) orthodontists are better than dentists.

(D) braces are not worth wearing.

3. Which statement shows a personal connection to the text?

(A) My dad tells jokes, too.

(B) I got braces and it took me a while to get used to them, too.

(C) I don't like ice cream.

(D) My haircut appointment is tomorrow.

4. How did Claire change?

(A) She was angry at her mom but then forgave her.

(B) She was afraid of the dentist but then she was brave.

(C) She refused to brush her teeth but then changed her mind.

(D) She was dreading having braces but later realized they would help her get a beautiful smile.

5. What message does this text share about making a change?

(A) Parents can't make you not worry.

(B) Everyone should reward themselves with ice cream.

(C) Going to the dentist for something new is scary.

(D) It may take time to get used to something new, but it will end up being okay.

6. Which title indicates a similar text?

(A) My New Eyeglasses

(B) Going to School

(C) A Bad Sleepover

(D) A Fun Time

1. (Y)(N)

2. (Y)(N)

3. (Y)(N)

4. (Y)(N)

5. (Y)(N)

6. (Y)(N)

___ / 6

Total

NAME:_____ **DATE:**_____

DIRECTIONS Reread "A New Kind of Smile." Then, read the prompt and respond on the lines below.

Braces are a big change for anyone. Claire worried that this new change was going to be hard to live with for a while. Write about a time when have you been worried about a change in your life.

_____

_____

_____

_____

_____

_____

_____

_____

_____

_____

_____

_____

_____

_____

_____

NAME:_____ DATE:_____

DIRECTIONS Read the text and then answer the questions.

John Glenn is a famous astronaut. He was the first to orbit Earth. He orbited our planet three times. It took about five hours. Glenn did not slow down after his space travels. He continued to serve his country. He was a senator for almost twenty-five years! Glenn also became the oldest person to travel into space. He went up when he was seventy-seven. John Glenn is an American hero.

1. Ⓨ Ⓝ

2. Ⓨ Ⓝ

3. Ⓨ Ⓝ

1. Which question about the text would help readers monitor their reading?

Ⓐ Where is the country?

Ⓑ How do people travel?

Ⓒ How many times did we run around the playground?

Ⓓ Who is John Glenn?

2. Which title best fits this text?

Ⓐ Up in Space

Ⓑ Space Travel

Ⓒ John Glenn, An American Hero

Ⓓ Planets in Orbit

3. Which word has the same vowel sound as *space*?

Ⓐ travel

Ⓑ planet

Ⓒ track

Ⓓ fate

4. What is the definition of *serve* as it is used in this text?

Ⓐ supply

Ⓑ work for

Ⓒ wait

Ⓓ give food

4. Ⓨ Ⓝ

5. Ⓨ Ⓝ

5. Which word describes the tone of this text?

Ⓐ factual

Ⓑ warning

Ⓒ funny

Ⓓ persuasive

___ / 5
Total

NAME: _____ DATE: _____

DIRECTIONS Read the text and then answer the questions.

1. Ⓨ Ⓝ

2. Ⓨ Ⓝ

    Space travel is amazing. People support the missions to space. They think of astronauts as heroes. Yet some missions have not been successful. Some have been tragedies. There have been accidents. Astronauts have been injured. Some have even died. These are such huge losses. The entire world feels sad when a space crew does not make it home.

3. Ⓨ Ⓝ

1. What does the first sentence tell about this text?

Ⓐ It is about space travel.

Ⓑ It is about amazing things.

4. Ⓨ Ⓝ

Ⓒ It is about countries.

Ⓓ It is about accidents.

5. Ⓨ Ⓝ

3. Which two words from the text have the same vowel sound?

Ⓐ *such* and *huge*

Ⓑ *died* and *it*

Ⓒ *sad* and *have*

Ⓓ *when* and *does*

___ / 5
Total

2. Which chapter title would help a reader find this information in a table of contents?

Ⓐ Huge Losses

Ⓑ Tragic Times

Ⓒ Risky Space Travel

Ⓓ Following the Mission

4. Which word is a synonym for *tragedies*?

Ⓐ missions

Ⓑ disasters

Ⓒ trips

Ⓓ moments

5. What other type of text is most similar to this text?

Ⓐ a math workbook

Ⓑ a story about airplanes

Ⓒ a letter

Ⓓ a history textbook

NAME:_____ DATE:_____

DIRECTIONS Read the text and then answer the questions.

SCORE

We have come a long way with space travel. Yet there are many places that we still cannot explore. These are places that are too hot or too cold. Other planets are either too close or too far from the sun. This causes conditions that make it impossible for humans to survive. Instead, we send robots to go and explore some of these areas. Perhaps a day will come when humans will be able to land on other planets.

1. (Y)(N)

2. (Y)(N)

3. (Y)(N)

1. Which type of image would tell a reader more about this text?

Ⓐ a sketch of the sun

Ⓑ a picture of a sunset

Ⓒ a photograph of an astronaut

Ⓓ a photograph of a robot on a space mission

2. Which index entry would help a reader find this information in a book?

Ⓐ moons

Ⓑ robots in space

Ⓒ survival skills

Ⓓ all of the above

3. Which word makes a new word by adding the prefix re–?

Ⓐ send

Ⓑ areas

Ⓒ day

Ⓓ when

4. (Y)(N)

5. (Y)(N)

4. Which word has the same root word as *impossible*?

Ⓐ pose

Ⓑ possibility

Ⓒ posse

Ⓓ important

___ / 5

Total

5. Which word describes the tone of this text?

Ⓐ inspiring

Ⓑ warning

Ⓒ sad

Ⓓ informative

NAME: _____ DATE: _____

To the Moon and Beyond!

Space is an endless world for people to explore. Humans have learned a lot in the past decades. We will never know all there is to know about space. We still have more to learn.

Man's first exploration into space began in 1957. A satellite was sent into space. It orbited Earth. It stayed there for three months. The next plan was for humans to go up in space. First, a few animals were sent up to see what would happen. Scientists were able to observe the effects of space on living things.

NASA was formed in 1958. NASA stands for the National Aeronautics and Space Administration. NASA organizes ways to travel to and study space. It also trains astronauts. At first, astronauts went up to orbit Earth. They wanted to take a longer trip in space. NASA was finally ready. The mission was called *Project Apollo*. This was going to send a man to the moon. It finally happened! The date was July 20, 1969. Astronauts landed on the moon. They walked on it for the first time. Neil Armstrong walked on the moon first and made a famous statement. He said, "That's one small step for man, one giant leap for mankind."

NASA made changes to its space program. It began to build space shuttles. They could be used again and again. This was new technology for space travel. Many trips have been taken in shuttles. Each expedition teaches us more about the world beyond our skies.

Today one of NASA's focuses is the International Space Station. It is almost like a city in space. There are people there from many countries. They are all trying to study space. They want to learn about life in space. Perhaps humans will be in space for long periods of time. Who knows what the future holds? The sky is not the limit on space travel!

Space Shuttle Atlantis launch

NAME:_____ DATE:_____

DIRECTIONS Read "To the Moon and Beyond!" and then answer the questions.

1. What is the purpose for reading this text?

Ⓐ to be entertained

Ⓑ to be persuaded to become an astronaut

Ⓒ to learn about Neil Armstrong's life

Ⓓ to learn about space travel

2. Which statement would the author likely agree with?

Ⓐ Space travel is dangerous.

Ⓑ Space travel has an exciting future.

Ⓒ Space travel is in the past.

Ⓓ Space travel is too expensive.

3. Who might easily relate to this text?

Ⓐ a child who likes to swing high at the playground

Ⓑ a person who likes to drive his car

Ⓒ a child who loves her telescope and watches the stars

Ⓓ a teacher who is teaching a unit on air pollution

4. How is this text organized?

Ⓐ as a comparison of space travel and air travel

Ⓑ as a chronological history of space travel

Ⓒ as a list of steps for how to become an astronaut

Ⓓ as a chronological history of how the universe was formed

5. What is the main point of this text?

Ⓐ Space travel only goes to the space station.

Ⓑ Space travel lets us explore unknown worlds.

Ⓒ Space travel is about going to the moon.

Ⓓ Space travel will end when people live in space.

6. What will happen in the future with space travel?

Ⓐ We will all live in space.

Ⓑ No one really knows.

Ⓒ We will discover alien life somewhere.

Ⓓ We will discover other life forms in another universe.

1. Ⓨ Ⓝ

2. Ⓨ Ⓝ

3. Ⓨ Ⓝ

4. Ⓨ Ⓝ

5. Ⓨ Ⓝ

6. Ⓨ Ⓝ

___ / 6
Total

NAME: _____ DATE: _____

DIRECTIONS Reread "To the Moon and Beyond!" Then, read the prompt and respond on the lines below.

Space travel has been an amazing advancement for mankind. Would you ever want to travel into space? Why or why not?

_____

_____

_____

_____

_____

_____

_____

_____

_____

_____

_____

_____

_____

_____

_____

_____

NAME: _____ **DATE:** _____

DIRECTIONS   Read the text and then answer the questions.

Jackson wondered what life would be like on the road with a band. His uncle is a sound engineer who goes on tour with a popular rock band. He is called a *roadie*, which is short for road crew. He is someone who travels with and works for a band to make sure they sound great during a concert. What an interesting job!

1. Ⓨ Ⓝ

2. Ⓨ Ⓝ

3. Ⓨ Ⓝ

4. Ⓨ Ⓝ

5. Ⓨ Ⓝ

___ / 5

Total

1. Which title would tell a reader more about this text?

Ⓐ Rock and Roll

Ⓑ The Life of a Roadie

Ⓒ Amazing Jobs

Ⓓ A Great Sound

2. What is the conflict in the text?

Ⓐ Jackson wants to go on tour with his uncle but he has to go to school instead.

Ⓑ Jackson's uncle wants a new job but can't find the courage to quit.

Ⓒ Jackson wants to play in a band but doesn't know how to play any instruments.

Ⓓ There is no conflict.

3. Which word has the same vowel sound as *road*?

Ⓐ tour

Ⓑ know

Ⓒ hop

Ⓓ cow

4. Which definition of *short* is used in this text?

Ⓐ rude

Ⓑ not long

Ⓒ not tall

Ⓓ abbreviated

5. What is *roadie* short for?

Ⓐ roadwork

Ⓑ engineer

Ⓒ road crew

Ⓓ roads

NAME: _____ DATE: _____

DIRECTIONS Read the text and then answer the questions.

SCORE

1. Ⓨ Ⓝ

2. Ⓨ Ⓝ

3. Ⓨ Ⓝ

4. Ⓨ Ⓝ

5. Ⓨ Ⓝ

___ / 5
Total

The radio disc jockey is tired after working the graveyard shift. He works at night. Most people are at home in bed. Not everyone is asleep, though. The disc jockey plays music for whoever is awake and listening. He likes to play music to balance out the quiet at night.

1. Which is an accurate summary of this text?

Ⓐ It is about people sleeping at night.

Ⓑ It is about a disc jockey who works at night.

Ⓒ It is about keeping music quiet at night.

Ⓓ It is about visiting a graveyard.

2. The main character works at a

Ⓐ graveyard.

Ⓑ radio station.

Ⓒ music store.

Ⓓ race track.

3. Which word is the root word in *listening*?

Ⓐ list

Ⓑ ing

Ⓒ ten

Ⓓ listen

4. What does it mean to work a *graveyard shift*?

Ⓐ to work all night

Ⓑ to work all day

Ⓒ not to work at all

Ⓓ to work at a cemetery

5. What does the phrase *to balance out* mean in the text?

Ⓐ use a scale

Ⓑ make two things work together

Ⓒ add up

Ⓓ weigh

NAME: _____ **DATE:** _____

DIRECTIONS Read the text and then answer the questions.

   Frank was angry with his father. He told Frank to mow the lawn before going swimming with his friends, but Frank did not want to do it. He resented having his dad always tell him what to do. Frank wondered when he would be on his own. He was tired of having to answer to his father all the time.

1. Ⓨ Ⓝ

2. Ⓨ Ⓝ

3. Ⓨ Ⓝ

1. Which picture would tell a reader more about this text?

Ⓐ a picture of an angry boy

Ⓑ a picture of a swimming pool

Ⓒ a picture of two happy parents

Ⓓ a picture of a lawn mower

4. Which is a synonym for *tired* as it is used in this text?

Ⓐ exhausted

Ⓑ annoyed with

Ⓒ worn out

Ⓓ overused

4. Ⓨ Ⓝ

5. Ⓨ Ⓝ

2. Which word best describes the main character?

Ⓐ sad

Ⓑ silly

Ⓒ frustrated

Ⓓ quiet

5. Which of the following similes applies to Frank?

Ⓐ as angry as a hive of bees

Ⓑ as tall as a tree

Ⓒ moved like a bear

Ⓓ sounded like a whisper

___ / 5

Total

3. How many syllables are in the word *resented*?

Ⓐ one syllable

Ⓑ two syllables

Ⓒ three syllables

Ⓓ four syllables

NAME:_____ DATE:_____

Concert Tickets

Maddy could not believe that Jared Baxter was coming to her town. He was playing a concert at the large arena downtown, and she really wanted to go! Maddy did not think anyone else was a bigger Jared Baxter fan than she was, and she had never seen him perform live. This was his second world tour, but she had been too young to go to his show last year. Now she knew all his songs and watched his videos all the time, so she just had to go to the show!

She knew that getting her parents to say yes would be no easy task. The concert was on a school night, and one of them would have to go with her. Plus, she really wanted to take Lily and Dana with her, so she had to get three sets of parents to say yes.

"Mom? Dad? I need to ask you something. I really want to go to the Jared Baxter show," Maddy began. "I have saved up my allowance so I can buy the ticket myself. I know that Lily and Dana can buy their tickets, too. I know I have never been to a concert, but this is really important to me." Maddy stayed calm because she wanted to show her parents that she was serious.

"It's on a school night," replied her mom. "That is going to make it pretty hard that week. Will you still have time for homework and piano practice?"

"I promise to do both! Can I please buy the tickets?" Maddy begged.

"Well, as long as Lily and Dana can go. Have their mothers call me," Maddy's mom explained. "And then we will go."

Maddy's scream could be heard by all the neighbors. She was so excited. Now her biggest problem would be waiting for the day of the show to arrive!

#50924—180 Days of Reading for Third Grade   © Shell Education

NAME: _____ **DATE:** _____

DIRECTIONS Read "Concert Tickets" and then answer the questions.

1. Which summary of the text is the most accurate?

(A) A band sells tickets to raise money for an important cause.

(B) A young person wants concert tickets.

(C) A school sells tickets for a concert.

(D) A character is worried about having money for tickets.

2. What is the author's purpose?

(A) to share Jared Baxter's music

(B) to entertain with a story about getting to go to a concert

(C) to teach about the increase in concert ticket prices

(D) to have readers solve math problems about money

3. Which shows a personal connection to the text?

(A) I went to a movie with my parents last night.

(B) My friends are all in a band.

(C) I don't really like concerts.

(D) I begged my parents to let me have a sleepover and they said yes.

4. Which word describes Maddy's feelings at the end of the text?

(A) thrilled

(B) frustrated

(C) angered

(D) scared

5. What can readers learn from Maddy's actions?

(A) Showing your parents that you are responsible and mature can help you get what you want.

(B) Going to a concert alone is no fun.

(C) Parents don't remember what it is like to be a kid.

(D) Showing your parents how excited you are can be a bad plan.

6. Which other type of text is similar to this text?

(A) a poem about parents and kids

(B) a newspaper advertising concert tickets for sale

(C) a fictional story about a boy who wants to go skiing and asks his parents

(D) a magazine article about Jared Baxter

1. (Y)(N)

2. (Y)(N)

3. (Y)(N)

4. (Y)(N)

5. (Y)(N)

6. (Y)(N)

___ / 6

Total

SCORE

___ / 4

NAME: _____ **DATE:** _____

DIRECTIONS Reread "Concert Tickets." Then, read the prompt and respond on the lines below.

Think about a time that you asked a family member for something that was important to you. How did you ask your important question, and what was the answer?

_____

_____

_____

_____

_____

_____

_____

_____

_____

_____

_____

_____

_____

_____

NAME:_____ DATE:_____

DIRECTIONS Read the text and then answer the questions.

Earth's surface is always changing. Change can happen quickly. A landslide is one example. The ground moves and the surface slips down a slope. The surface is changed in a moment. Sometimes, change happens much more slowly. *Erosion* is a slow process. Rock or soil gradually wear away. This is caused by water, wind, or ice. This changes the surface.

1. Ⓨ Ⓝ

2. Ⓨ Ⓝ

3. Ⓨ Ⓝ

1. What is this text about?

Ⓐ This text is about how land moves and changes.

Ⓑ This text is about volcanoes.

Ⓒ This text is about Earth's changing temperatures.

Ⓓ This text is about oceans.

3. Which word has the same root word as *quickly*?

Ⓐ quiz

Ⓑ sickly

Ⓒ quicken

Ⓓ quilt

4. Ⓨ Ⓝ

5. Ⓨ Ⓝ

2. Which title best fits this text?

Ⓐ Erosion

Ⓑ Earth's Changes: Quick and Slow

Ⓒ Wearing Away

Ⓓ Quick Changes

4. Which is a synonym of *gradually*?

Ⓐ quickly

Ⓑ slowly

Ⓒ mysteriously

Ⓓ incredibly

___ / 5
Total

5. What does the phrase *in a moment* mean?

Ⓐ quickly

Ⓑ in one hour

Ⓒ in one minute

Ⓓ soon enough

NAME: _____ DATE: _____

DIRECTIONS Read the text and then answer the questions.

1. Ⓨ Ⓝ

2. Ⓨ Ⓝ

3. Ⓨ Ⓝ

4. Ⓨ Ⓝ

5. Ⓨ Ⓝ

___ / 5
Total

> A canyon is a type of landform. The Grand Canyon is very famous. It is in Arizona. It was formed by a river. The Colorado River runs through the canyon. It is home to many plants and animals. The diverse habitat is unique. The canyon has amazing natural beauty. People enjoy looking at the view. The view is worth the visit. People come from all over the world to see the Grand Canyon.

1. Which title best fits this text?

Ⓐ The Grand Canyon

Ⓑ Many Visitors

Ⓒ Arizona Sites

Ⓓ Amazing Habitats

2. Where is the Grand Canyon located?

Ⓐ Colorado

Ⓑ in a river

Ⓒ in a canyon

Ⓓ Arizona

3. Which word has the same root word as *amazing*?

Ⓐ amount

Ⓑ amazed

Ⓒ maze

Ⓓ hazing

4. What is an antonym of *unique*?

Ⓐ common

Ⓑ rare

Ⓒ beautiful

Ⓓ active

5. Which word from the text tells the reader that the Grand Canyon is one-of-a-kind?

Ⓐ landform

Ⓑ unique

Ⓒ beauty

Ⓓ view

NAME:_____ DATE:_____

DIRECTIONS Read the text and then answer the questions.

Lakes come in all sizes and shapes. They also differ in the kind of water they contain. Some lakes are freshwater lakes, and others are *saline*. This means they are full of saltwater. A large saltwater lake is also called a sea. The Dead Sea is a famous body of water. It gets its name because animals cannot live in water that is so high in salt.

1. Ⓨ Ⓝ

2. Ⓨ Ⓝ

3. Ⓨ Ⓝ

4. Ⓨ Ⓝ

5. Ⓨ Ⓝ

___ / 5

Total

1. Which is the best summary of the text?

Ⓐ This text is about different types of lakes.

Ⓑ This text is about saltwater.

Ⓒ This text is about seas.

Ⓓ This text is about salt.

2. Which title best fits this text?

Ⓐ Saltwater Lakes

Ⓑ Kinds of Lakes

Ⓒ Saline in Water

Ⓓ Freshwater Lakes

3. What word from the text can make a new word with the prefix *re–*?

Ⓐ kind

Ⓑ sea

Ⓒ water

Ⓓ called

4. Which of these words mean the same thing?

Ⓐ *full* and *name*

Ⓑ *live* and *body*

Ⓒ *large* and *water*

Ⓓ *saltwater* and *saline*

5. What does it mean to *come in all sizes and shapes*?

Ⓐ to be really big

Ⓑ to need to be measured

Ⓒ to be hard to define

Ⓓ have different kinds

NAME:_____ DATE:_____

Facts About Landforms

A *landform* is a natural formation of rock and dirt found on Earth. Landforms come in all shapes and sizes. They include entire mountain ranges and small hills. A landform might be as large as a continent or as small as a pond. Landforms are made by some kind of a force of nature. This force could be wind, water, or ice.

Many landforms are shaped by water. Valleys and canyons are similar landforms. How are they different? Canyons are more narrow and surrounded by steep sides. Valleys are situated between hills or mountains. A *delta* is another landform created by water. Deltas can be found at the mouths of rivers. They are triangle-shaped. They are created when sand, silt, and rock accumulate.

Mountains are usually part of a range or chain.

Hills and mountains are landforms. A hill is raised, sloped land. A mountain is usually higher, with a definite peak. *Mesas* are part of this group, too. They are known as table mountains. They are elevated like mountains but with flat tops and steep sides. Mesas are formed by erosion and weathering.

The opposite of these raised forms are the plains. Plains are landforms that are flat and broad. Plains have a low elevation.

Landforms help us describe land areas in a more accurate way. Which landforms are near where you live?

NAME:_____ **DATE:**_____

DIRECTIONS Read "Facts About Landforms" and then answer the questions.

SCORE

1. Which summary of the text is most accurate?

(A) It tells when landforms were made.

(B) It includes facts about landforms.

(C) It describes the most famous landforms.

(D) It describes landforms around the world.

2. What is a purpose for reading this text?

(A) to compare two similar things

(B) to be persuaded to accept a viewpoint

(C) to be entertained

(D) to learn new facts and information

3. Who would likely have prior knowledge related to this text?

(A) a scientist who studies weather

(B) a person who lives on a hill

(C) a person who has visited different types of landforms

(D) a person who enjoys skiing

4. Which statement accurately describes how the text is organized?

(A) The history of landforms is described in chronological order.

(B) How landforms are formed is described in sequential order.

(C) Similar types of landforms are explained and compared.

(D) The text is not organized at all.

5. What is the main idea?

(A) Landforms are all unique and interesting.

(B) Landforms are made by ice.

(C) Landforms involve water.

(D) Landforms are at low elevations.

6. Which landform is **not** discussed in this text?

(A) deltas

(B) glaciers

(C) mountains

(D) plains

1. (Y)(N)

2. (Y)(N)

3. (Y)(N)

4. (Y)(N)

5. (Y)(N)

6. (Y)(N)

___ / 6
Total

NAME: _____ **DATE:** _____

DIRECTIONS Reread "Facts About Landforms." Then, read the prompt and respond on the lines below.

Review the landforms that are mentioned in the text. Which landforms are you most familiar with? Which landforms would you like to visit?

_____

_____

_____

_____

_____

_____

_____

_____

_____

_____

_____

_____

_____

_____

_____

NAME:_____ DATE:_____

DIRECTIONS Read the text and then answer the questions.

I rushed out of the house and ran to get my bike as my mom called for me. "Not so fast, Jessie!" she shouted. "Don't forget your helmet!" I was only riding up the street to my friend's house, but I guess it doesn't matter how far I am riding. I have to wear a helmet no matter what because it keeps me safe. There is even a law in my town that requires children to wear bike helmets.

1. Y N

2. Y N

3. Y N

4. Y N

5. Y N

1. Which phrase would tell a reader more about this text while previewing it?

- (A) a law in my town
- (B) a helmet no matter what
- (C) my mom called for me
- (D) up the street

2. Who is the narrator?

- (A) Jessie's friend
- (B) Jessie's mom
- (C) Jessie
- (D) Jessie's dad

3. Which word from the text has the same vowel sound as *talk*?

- (A) safe
- (B) how
- (C) law
- (D) bike

4. Which is a synonym for *requires*?

- (A) hopes
- (B) demands
- (C) wishes
- (D) grabs

5. Which phrase shows how Jessie feels about wearing a helmet?

- (A) have to wear a helmet no matter what
- (B) get my bike
- (C) riding up the street
- (D) requires children to wear bike helmets

___ / 5
Total

NAME:_____ DATE:_____

DIRECTIONS   Read the text and then answer the questions.

1. Y N

2. Y N

Luis wanted to ride his bike around the neighborhood. His dad told him to ride with Marco, his little brother. The problem was that Marco was still riding a bike with training wheels. He was going to slow Luis down, and Luis did not want that. He wanted to go as fast as he could. He tried to change the plan, but his dad insisted so Luis had no choice. He was not going to get the kind of bike ride that he wanted.

3. Y N

1. Which title best fits this text?

   Ⓐ   Slowed Down by a Brother

4. Y N

   Ⓑ   A Bike Ride

   Ⓒ   Around the Neighborhood

5. Y N

   Ⓓ   Luis and Marco

____ / 5

Total

2. Which word best describes the main character at the end of the text?

   Ⓐ   disappointed

   Ⓑ   excited

   Ⓒ   happy

   Ⓓ   tired

3. Which word has the same vowel sound as *ride*?

   Ⓐ   rid

   Ⓑ   fly

   Ⓒ   hid

   Ⓓ   tip

4. Which word is a synonym for *choice*?

   Ⓐ   work

   Ⓑ   time

   Ⓒ   option

   Ⓓ   direction

5. What does the text's tone tell the reader about how it ends?

   Ⓐ   Luis is excited that things have changed.

   Ⓑ   Luis has to accept the new plan, even if he doesn't want to.

   Ⓒ   Marco feels bad to slow down his brother.

   Ⓓ   Luis's father is frustrated with both boys.

NAME:_____ DATE:_____

DIRECTIONS Read the text and then answer the questions.

    The girls were riding their bikes home from school. It was a new experience for them. They were starting to ride by themselves without an adult. They were being very responsible. Suddenly, one of the bikes had a problem. It was a flat tire, and the girls were still about a mile from home. What were they supposed to do? They stayed calm, and decided to walk their bikes home together and fix the flat tire at home.

1. Ⓨ Ⓝ

2. Ⓨ Ⓝ

3. Ⓨ Ⓝ

1. Which best summarizes this text?

Ⓐ It is about girls being responsible and solving a problem.

Ⓑ It is about how to change a bike tire.

Ⓒ It is about girls getting lost.

Ⓓ It is about girls not following rules.

2. What is the setting?

Ⓐ a playground

Ⓑ a neighborhood

Ⓒ a school

Ⓓ a house

3. Which word is the root word in *riding*?

Ⓐ ding

Ⓑ ride

Ⓒ rid

Ⓓ ridi

4. Ⓨ Ⓝ

5. Ⓨ Ⓝ

4. Which word from the text means *reliable*?

Ⓐ decided

Ⓑ experience

Ⓒ calm

Ⓓ responsible

___/ 5
Total

5. What does the word *suddenly* tell the reader about an event?

Ⓐ Someone gets hurt.

Ⓑ Something happens that is surprising.

Ⓒ Something happens slowly.

Ⓓ Something happens that is exciting.

NAME: _____ DATE: _____

Making Room for Bikes

January 20, 2012

Dear Mayor,

I am writing to you about a serious problem in our town. I think it is important to have clearly marked bike lanes on our busiest streets. Something happened yesterday that made me write this letter. I was riding my bike home from school. I was with my mom and my sister. We were going north on Lakeview Drive. The three of us were on the right side of the road. We were following all the rules of the road. We were all wearing helmets. We were using clear hand signals. All of a sudden, a large car turned right into our path! Luckily, I was able to stop right away. My mother and sister were behind me. They could stop, too. It was a close call. This driver almost hit me and my bike.

I was in the right place on the road. Yet this driver did not see me. I think that if I had been riding inside a very clearly marked bike lane, then I would have been more visible. There are many of us in our community who ride bikes. Our safety on the roads is important.

Our school has been talking a lot about healthy choices. We have discussed good nutrition. We have talked about how important it is to move our bodies each day. We have even started to make changes at our own school. Our cafeteria serves a lot of yummy fruits and vegetables! If health is so important, riding a bike is a great idea. It is an easy and fun form of exercise. I think we want to encourage people to do this. If people are worried about being hurt on the road, they will be less likely to get on their bikes.

Please consider making this change around town. Make it easier for bicyclists to travel safely. Encourage people to get out of their cars and be healthy. Thank you.

Sincerely,

Josh Parker

NAME:_____ DATE:_____

DIRECTIONS Read "Making Room for Bikes" and then answer the questions.

1. Which summary of the letter is the most accurate?

Ⓐ This is about how bikes can be taken on city buses.

Ⓑ This is about keeping bikes safe.

Ⓒ This is about having safe places to ride bikes.

Ⓓ This is about people making time for exercise.

2. What is the author's purpose?

Ⓐ to make biking around town safer

Ⓑ to get rid of bike lanes

Ⓒ to get donations to improve cafeteria food

Ⓓ to find his stolen bike

3. How does this letter show a personal connection to the topic of bike safety?

Ⓐ The author has been in cars that have had problems with bicyclists.

Ⓑ The author shares his own experience with bike safety.

Ⓒ The author has interviewed a lot of bike riders.

Ⓓ The author is an expert cyclist.

4. Which statement is true about the author?

Ⓐ He thinks bikers are dangerous to cars.

Ⓑ He is upset because too many people drive cars.

Ⓒ He is happy to see bikers and cars traveling safely together.

Ⓓ He is upset because he and his family were almost hit by a car.

5. What message does this letter share about bike safety?

Ⓐ All bicyclists need flags on their bike.

Ⓑ Cars won't see bike riders unless they are wearing helmets.

Ⓒ Cars are more important than bicyclists.

Ⓓ Bicyclists deserve to be safe on the roads.

6. Which title indicates a similar type of text?

Ⓐ Space Invaders

Ⓑ A Day at the Beach

Ⓒ Staying Safe

Ⓓ Getting Along with Siblings

1. Ⓨ Ⓝ

2. Ⓨ Ⓝ

3. Ⓨ Ⓝ

4. Ⓨ Ⓝ

5. Ⓨ Ⓝ

6. Ⓨ Ⓝ

___ / 6
Total

SCORE

___ / 4

NAME:_____ DATE:_____

DIRECTIONS Reread the text "Making Room for Bikes." Then, read the prompt and respond on the lines below.

Think about an issue in your city or town. What would you write about to the mayor?

_____

_____

_____

_____

_____

_____

_____

_____

_____

_____

_____

_____

_____

_____

_____

NAME: _____ **DATE:** _____

DIRECTIONS Read the text and then answer the questions.

Insects can be very different. Some fly, while others walk or jump. Some insects help us while others harm us. Yet insects have some things in common. Insects are *invertebrates*, which means they have no backbone. All insects have the same three body parts: a head, an abdomen, and a thorax. Insects have three pairs of legs and two pairs of wings.

1. Ⓨ Ⓝ

2. Ⓨ Ⓝ

3. Ⓨ Ⓝ

1. Which question about the text would help readers monitor their reading?

Ⓐ Who has an abdomen?

Ⓑ How are insects different?

Ⓒ What would I do if I had wings?

Ⓓ Who has broken a bone?

2. Which title best describes the main idea of this text?

Ⓐ No Backbones

Ⓑ Insects

Ⓒ Fly or Walk?

Ⓓ Three Insect Parts

3. What suffix could you add to the root word *help* to make a new word?

Ⓐ –er

Ⓑ –ly

Ⓒ –est

Ⓓ –ion

4. What is an antonym for *harm*?

Ⓐ hate

Ⓑ hit

Ⓒ help

Ⓓ bite

5. Which word describes the tone of this text?

Ⓐ factual

Ⓑ angry

Ⓒ funny

Ⓓ persuasive

4. Ⓨ Ⓝ

5. Ⓨ Ⓝ

___ / 5

Total

NAME:_____ DATE:_____

SCORE

DIRECTIONS Read the text and then answer the questions.

1. Ⓨ Ⓝ

2. Ⓨ Ⓝ

Monarch butterflies eat plants. This makes them *herbivores*. Caterpillars only eat milkweed leaves. Adult monarchs like to drink nectar. They find nectar in milkweed. They also find it in other wildflowers. Garden flowers attract monarchs, too. People put certain plants in their garden. They hope to attract monarchs. They want to see them fly through!

3. Ⓨ Ⓝ

1. What does the first sentence tell about this text?

Ⓐ The text is about how monarchs migrate.

Ⓑ The text is about how monarchs navigate.

Ⓒ The text is about what monarchs eat.

Ⓓ The text is about plants that monarchs live in.

4. Ⓨ Ⓝ

5. Ⓨ Ⓝ

___/ 5
Total

2. Which index entry would help a reader find this information?

Ⓐ milkweed leaves

Ⓑ nectar

Ⓒ diet of monarchs

Ⓓ all of the above

3. Which word has the same root word as *plants*?

Ⓐ pants

Ⓑ planting

Ⓒ ant

Ⓓ ants

4. What does *attract* mean in this text?

Ⓐ see clearly

Ⓑ hear clearly

Ⓒ bring in

Ⓓ match closely

5. Where might this text be found?

Ⓐ a joke book

Ⓑ a book of poetry

Ⓒ a newspaper

Ⓓ a science textbook

NAME:_____ DATE:_____

DIRECTIONS Read the text and then answer the questions.

Monarch butterflies have different names. The word *monarch* means king or queen. Monarch butterflies used to be called *King Billy*. This was a name after the king of England. Today, they are also known as *milkweed butterflies*. Some people call them *wanderers*. The name does not matter. These insects are beautiful!

1. (Y) (N)

2. (Y) (N)

3. (Y) (N)

1. Which question about the text would help readers monitor their reading?

(A) What stories have a king or queen?

(B) Who is a wanderer?

(C) What are different names for monarch butterflies?

(D) Where is England?

2. Which chapter heading would help a reader find this text in a book?

(A) King Billy

(B) Names for Monarch Butterflies

(C) Word Meanings

(D) Beautiful Insects

3. Which word from the text makes a new word by adding the prefix *re–*?

(A) king

(B) name

(C) matter

(D) them

4. Which of these words is a synonym of *monarch*?

(A) wanderer

(B) emperor

(C) milkweed

(D) march

4. (Y) (N)

5. (Y) (N)

5. What does the language of this text tell you about the author's purpose?

(A) The language is personal so that people will feel like having their own butterfly.

(B) The language is factual so that people will learn more about butterflies.

(C) The language is funny so that people will laugh about butterflies.

(D) The language is persuasive so that people will have new opinions about butterflies.

___ / 5
Total

NAME:_____ DATE:_____

Monarch Butterflies

Monarch butterflies are stunning. Their colors and patterns are beautiful. They are easy to spot as they fly through the air. Adult monarchs start life as an egg. Then, they hatch as a caterpillar. That phase lasts for about two weeks. Then, the caterpillar creates a chrysalis (KRIS-uh-lis) or a hard shell. Changes take place. Soon, a butterfly emerges.

The monarch's bright colors are quite striking. Some people think the colors should attract predators. Yet they actually protect the butterfly from predators. This is called an *adaptation*. It is how an animal changes itself. These changes increase the odds of survival. This change begins when monarchs are caterpillars. Caterpillars eat milkweed leaves. These leaves have a poisonous chemical. The caterpillars store the chemical in their bodies. It does not harm them. It makes them taste horrible to predators. Predators do not want to eat them.

monarch butterfly

Monarchs migrate from a summer to a winter habitat. They may be the only butterfly species to do this. Most start their migration in September or October. They travel the same routes each year. The journey is divided by many stops. Each night, monarchs stop to rest or feed. They gather in a tree. This may be a eucalyptus tree. It could be a pine or a cypress. A single tree can have thousands of monarchs in it. This trip can take up to ninety days. This migration has caused problems, though.

The problem occurs when people cut down trees. The trees are *logged*. People use the wood for building. They want the open space, too. They want to build on the land. The monarchs can no longer take shelter in the trees. They cannot stop to rest. They cannot stay warm. They cannot keep from drying out.

Some people are trying to help monarchs. They are protecting their habitats. People are planting milkweed. They are planting other flowers. People want monarchs to have food and water. They also want them to have shelter. These things will keep this beautiful species alive.

 #50924—180 Days of Reading for Third Grade

NAME:_____ DATE:_____

DIRECTIONS Read "Monarch Butterflies" and then answer the questions.

1. What is the purpose for reading this text?

(A) to laugh about how silly butterflies are

(B) to be persuaded that butterflies are the best insects in the world

(C) to learn about monarch butterflies

(D) to learn about adaptations

2. How does the author feel about butterfly habitats being destroyed?

(A) It is a serious problem, and people are working to fix it.

(B) It is okay because more trees will grow.

(C) It should not matter because buildings are important.

(D) It is funny because the butterflies are so silly.

3. Which statement shows a connection to the text?

(A) I do not know what poison is.

(B) I have worked to save bird habitats.

(C) I have plants in my garden.

(D) I have seen a chicken lay an egg before.

4. Which topic is **not** covered in this text?

(A) how and where monarchs migrate

(B) how monarchs use their colors as an adaptation

(C) where monarchs get their name

(D) what is happening to the monarch habitat

5. Which is the best summary of the text?

(A) Monarch butterflies start their migration in the fall.

(B) Monarch butterflies are amazing creatures, and their habitats are in danger.

(C) Milkweed leaves have a poisonous chemical.

(D) Monarch butterflies start life as an egg.

6. Why are butterfly habitats in danger?

(A) Wildfires are breaking out.

(B) Air pollution has killed the butterflies.

(C) Trees are being cut down.

(D) Predators now live in their habitats.

1. (Y)(N)

2. (Y)(N)

3. (Y)(N)

4. (Y)(N)

5. (Y)(N)

6. (Y)(N)

___ / 6
Total

NAME: _____ **DATE:** _____

DIRECTIONS Reread "Monarch Butterflies." Then, read the prompt and respond on the lines below.

Think about how monarch butterflies are struggling in areas where trees are cut down. Why do you think the situation with butterflies should matter to us?

_____

_____

_____

_____

_____

_____

_____

_____

_____

_____

_____

_____

_____

_____

NAME: _____ **DATE:** _____

DIRECTIONS Read the text and then answer the questions.

Kevin and Drake stood in front of the grocery store. They were in the middle of a three-hour shift. The two boys were on the same soccer team, and their team was selling candy. They were trying to raise money to attend a big tournament. The money would pay for a bus to bring the players to the game. Kevin and Drake were working hard to sell candy and earn some cash!

1. Ⓨ Ⓝ

2. Ⓨ Ⓝ

3. Ⓨ Ⓝ

1. Which is the most accurate summary of this text?

Ⓐ It is about two boys selling candy.

Ⓑ It is about two boys playing soccer.

Ⓒ It is about two friends eating candy.

Ⓓ It is about two boys on a bus.

2. Which verb best describes the actions of the main characters?

Ⓐ playing

Ⓑ selling

Ⓒ arguing

Ⓓ kicking

3. What suffix could you add to the root word *sell* to make a new word?

Ⓐ –es

Ⓑ –ly

Ⓒ –tion

Ⓓ –er

4. Ⓨ Ⓝ

5. Ⓨ Ⓝ

4. What is a synonym for *tournament*?

Ⓐ show

Ⓑ competition

Ⓒ performance

Ⓓ fight

___ / 5

Total

5. When would you likely hear the word *shift*?

Ⓐ a child talking about going to the library

Ⓑ an adult talking about going to work

Ⓒ a teacher gathering a homework assignment

Ⓓ a student taking a test

NAME:_____ **DATE:**_____

DIRECTIONS Read the text and then answer the questions.

SCORE

1. Ⓨ Ⓝ

2. Ⓨ Ⓝ

3. Ⓨ Ⓝ

4. Ⓨ Ⓝ

5. Ⓨ Ⓝ

___ / 5
Total

The family was on a bike ride on a hot summer day. They turned the corner and rode along a quiet street for a few minutes. All of a sudden, they noticed a small group of kids outside with a table. They were selling lemonade. "Lemonade, 25 cents!" the kids shouted. What a perfect drink during a hot bike ride!

1. Which title best fits this text?

Ⓐ A Quiet Street

Ⓑ A Lemonade Stand

Ⓒ Out for a Ride

Ⓓ My Favorite Drink

2. What did the family do during their bike ride?

Ⓐ They stopped to buy lemonade.

Ⓑ They argued.

Ⓒ They got lost.

Ⓓ They complained.

3. Which word is the root word in *turned*?

Ⓐ ned

Ⓑ urn

Ⓒ ed

Ⓓ turn

4. Which word means *saw*?

Ⓐ turned

Ⓑ noticed

Ⓒ shouted

Ⓓ outside

5. What does the phrase *all of a sudden* mean?

Ⓐ slowly

Ⓑ something unexpected happens

Ⓒ secretly

Ⓓ a quick stop

NAME:_____ DATE:_____

DIRECTIONS Read the text and then answer the questions.

It was exciting to get my very first job. My first job was mowing lawns for my neighbor when I was eight. I had been helping my dad with our yard for a few years, and so I knew what to do. I printed some flyers and passed them around on my street. I was not sure what would happen, but was thrilled when three neighbors wanted my services! Earning that first bit of money was so exciting!

1. Ⓨ Ⓝ

2. Ⓨ Ⓝ

3. Ⓨ Ⓝ

1. Which title best fits this text?

Ⓐ Three Neighbors

Ⓑ My First Job

Ⓒ Helping Dad

Ⓓ Cutting Grass

2. Who is the narrator?

Ⓐ a father

Ⓑ a child older than eight years old

Ⓒ a five-year-old

Ⓓ a lawn mower

3. Which word has the same root word as *helping*?

Ⓐ yelping

Ⓑ helper

Ⓒ eating

Ⓓ held

4. Which meaning of *services* is used in this text?

Ⓐ help

Ⓑ money

Ⓒ advice

Ⓓ flyer

4. Ⓨ Ⓝ

5. Ⓨ Ⓝ

5. Which word tells the reader that this was a new experience for the narrator?

Ⓐ thrilled

Ⓑ first

Ⓒ earning

Ⓓ job

___ / 5

Total

NAME:_____ DATE:_____

Raising Money

Our class has been studying native trees this year. We are learning so much about how important trees are to the health of our planet. Yesterday, our teacher told us about a nearby arboretum. An *arboretum* is like a tree museum. Many different kinds of trees are planted there. Our class was very excited to go there on a field trip.

There was a problem, however. This field trip would cost a lot of money, and our teacher was not sure how to pay for it. Parents had already donated money for field trips. We needed to cover the cost of the bus and the tickets. Our class decided to brainstorm ideas. We wondered how we might earn enough money.

We made a list of ideas. Then we voted on our ideas to see which would be the most popular. A read-a-thon won by a landslide! Kids were excited about this plan. We talked about all the details. We decided on a day. We also designed a sign-up sheet. Each student shared it with friends and family. People would pay us based on how many pages we read. We would even wear pajamas to school on that day. That way, we could read and be comfortable. It sounded like so much fun!

I took my job very seriously. I passed my sign-up sheet to everyone I knew. I wanted to raise as much money as possible because I really wanted to see the trees at the arboretum. I got twenty-five signatures. I think I raised a lot of money.

The day of the read-a-thon finally came. We all wore our pajamas. We read for a few hours in a row. I got a little bit tired, but it was a fun way to earn money. At the end of the day, my teacher made the big announcement. We had earned enough for our trip! What a great fund-raiser!

NAME: _____ **DATE:** _____

DIRECTIONS Read "Raising Money" and then answer the questions.

1. Which purpose for reading this text is most appropriate?

(A) to learn about native trees

(B) to be inspired to raise money or achieve some other goal as a group

(C) to compare a read-a-thon to a walk-a-thon

(D) to learn rules for going on a field trip

2. What is the author's opinion?

(A) Working together can have amazing results.

(B) Field trips are not worth the cost.

(C) A school bus is always expensive.

(D) Reading is hard work.

3. Who would best relate to the narrator's experience?

(A) a teacher who is teaching about native birds

(B) a class that is raising money to donate to an important cause

(C) a school-bus owner

(D) a librarian who reads to children

4. Which statement is true about the narrator?

(A) The narrator is angry about raising money.

(B) The narrator really wants to go to the arboretum.

(C) The narrator does not believe the class can raise money.

(D) The narrator is scared to read for so long.

5. What is a theme of this text?

(A) Field trips are hard to plan.

(B) Anything is possible with teamwork.

(C) Money is a private matter.

(D) Teachers have all the answers for problems.

6. What other type of text is similar to this story?

(A) a poem about trees

(B) a nonfiction text about how to stay safe on a bus trip

(C) a letter to the editor of a newspaper about raising money for a new playground

(D) a fictional story about two friends who love to sing

1. (Y) (N)

2. (Y) (N)

3. (Y) (N)

4. (Y) (N)

5. (Y) (N)

6. (Y) (N)

___ / 6
Total

NAME: _____ **DATE:** _____

DIRECTIONS Reread "Raising Money." Then, read the prompt and respond on the lines below.

This story is about a group of kids who work together to reach a common goal. When have you worked with others to achieve a goal or make something happen?

_____

_____

_____

_____

_____

_____

_____

_____

_____

_____

_____

_____

_____

_____

NAME: _____ **DATE:** _____

DIRECTIONS Read the text and then answer the questions.

A scorekeeper is an important person in sports. This is someone who keeps the official score. This job requires a lot. The scorekeeper has to watch the game very closely. Things can happen very quickly. This person also tracks other statistics. Each player is watched closely. All of the official numbers are tallied. They are shared at the end of the game.

1. (Y)(N)

2. (Y)(N)

3. (Y)(N)

1. Which word best summarizes the topic of this text?

(A) player

(B) scorekeeper

(C) game

(D) job

4. What is the definition of *tracks* as it is used in this text?

(A) path

(B) rail

(C) follows

(D) songs

4. (Y)(N)

5. (Y)(N)

2. Which title best describes the main idea of this text?

(A) A Number's Game

(B) Watching Closely

(C) Adding It Up

(D) A Scorekeeper's Job

5. What type of text would have language similar to this text?

(A) an autobiography

(B) a history book

(C) a sports magazine

(D) a newspaper

___ / 5

Total

3. Which suffix could you add to the root word *watch* to make a new word?

(A) –es

(B) –ly

(C) –s

(D) –ion

NAME: _____ **DATE:** _____

DIRECTIONS Read the text and then answer the questions.

1. Ⓨ Ⓝ

2. Ⓨ Ⓝ

3. Ⓨ Ⓝ

4. Ⓨ Ⓝ

5. Ⓨ Ⓝ

___ / 5
Total

An *average* is a type of statistic. It is found with a group of numbers. What is the average value? It is found by adding a group of numbers. Then the total is divided by the amount of numbers. An average tells us what value is most common. A teacher might claim an average of twenty-five students are in class each day. Some days may have more students. Some days may have fewer. The average is what is typical.

1. What does the first sentence tell about this text?

Ⓐ It is about number patterns.

Ⓑ It is about averages and statistics.

Ⓒ It is about hating math.

Ⓓ It is about geometry.

2. Which chapter title would help a reader find this information in a table of contents?

Ⓐ Adding Numbers

Ⓑ Finding Averages

Ⓒ Typical Values

Ⓓ Challenging Word Problems

3. Which word has the same root word as *divided*?

Ⓐ video

Ⓑ dive

Ⓒ division

Ⓓ dove

4. Which word is a synonym for *claim*?

Ⓐ demand

Ⓑ state

Ⓒ receive

Ⓓ win

5. What type of text would include language similar to this text?

Ⓐ an encyclopedia

Ⓑ a book of poetry

Ⓒ a letter

Ⓓ a math textbook

NAME:_____ DATE:_____

DIRECTIONS Read the text and then answer the questions.

SCORE

1. Y N

2. Y N

3. Y N

4. Y N

5. Y N

___ / 5
Total

The game of baseball is exciting to follow because the action does not stop for nine innings. Players are trying hard to get hits and score runs for their team. They want to hit the ball well, and they also want to get on base because that leads to points scored. A home run is the best a player can do at bat. This means the ball is hit out of the park. A player scores after a home run, and if others are on base, they score, too.

1. Which picture would tell a reader more about this text?

A a picture of a baseball and bat

B a picture of a number

C a picture of a trophy

D a picture of a base

2. Which index entry would help a reader find this information?

A soccer rules

B hits in baseball

C types of baseball bats

D scorekeepers

3. Which word from the text makes a new word by adding the prefix *pre–*?

A game

B follow

C stop

D nine

4. Which word has the same root word as *scored*?

A core

B scoring

C scare

D oar

5. What is the tone of this text?

A romantic

B angry

C persuasive

D informative

NAME: _____ DATE: _____

What Are Those Stats?

Many people love the game of baseball. Some people enjoy playing the sport. Others enjoy watching the game. Many fans love to do both!

The rules of the game are simple. The score tells people who is winning. Yet that is not the only number used in the game. Baseball statistics use a lot of numbers and math. They give us data about the game.

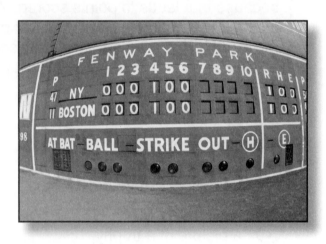

Statistics, or stats, do not always matter to fans. Some people only want to know how a team is doing. They follow the final score of games. They also know about the *standings*. This is the ranking of a team compared to other teams. Knowing your team is in first place is enough for many fans.

Other fans want more specific information. Fans may want to compare players. Using stats is a way to rank a player. Which common stats do people follow? One is the number of hits a player has. How often a player makes a hit tells us about how well he is playing. So does his *batting average*. This number shows how often a player hits a ball during a season. Have you heard of an RBI? That stands for a *run batted in*. This is another important stat. It tells us how much a player helps his team score.

Sometimes stats are important to fans for a short time. This happens when a player is getting close to breaking a record. For example, a strong hitter may hit many home runs over his career. The player then might get close to the record for most home runs. People will start to pay attention. They will watch games to see if that player will change his statistics. It becomes a countdown. People focus on the statistic. Breaking a record in any sport is a very big deal! Without statistics, there wouldn't be records to break!

Every time a player is up to bat, someone is watching. People are keeping score. They are also recording the events of the game. These become the record of a team's season. These records are kept forever. Statistics tell the story of a game. They tell the story of a player's performance. They are what baseball is all about.

NAME:_____ DATE:_____

DIRECTIONS Read "What Are Those Stats?" and then answer the questions.

1. Which is the best summary of the text?

Ⓐ It is about the importance of statistics in sports.

Ⓑ It is about how to calculate statistics.

Ⓒ It is about which players have the best statistics.

Ⓓ It is about what coaches do to get better statistics.

2. How does this author likely feel about math?

Ⓐ Math makes baseball boring.

Ⓑ Math is important in baseball.

Ⓒ Statistics are not relevant to our daily lives.

Ⓓ Math should only be studied in school.

3. Which shows a personal connection to the text?

Ⓐ I prefer team sports because they are more fun to play.

Ⓑ I always try to beat my best record on my swim team.

Ⓒ I worked with my math flash cards last night.

Ⓓ Our choir came in first place in yesterday's competition.

4. Which topic is **not** covered in this text?

Ⓐ what an RBI is

Ⓑ why statistics are interesting to baseball fans

Ⓒ who has the best statistics on today's baseball teams

Ⓓ why people pay close attention to certain stats when records might be broken

5. What is the main idea?

Ⓐ Being in first place is important to all fans.

Ⓑ Statistics tell us more about the game of baseball.

Ⓒ Statistics distract people from the action of the game.

Ⓓ Math has no place in sports.

6. What is an *RBI*?

Ⓐ run by inning

Ⓑ run batted in

Ⓒ real batting incident

Ⓓ run by incident

1. Ⓨ Ⓝ

2. Ⓨ Ⓝ

3. Ⓨ Ⓝ

4. Ⓨ Ⓝ

5. Ⓨ Ⓝ

6. Ⓨ Ⓝ

___ / 6

Total

NAME: _____ DATE: _____

DIRECTIONS Reread "What Are Those Stats?" Then, read the prompt and respond on the lines below.

Think about whether you would like to know these certain statistics as you watch a baseball game. Do you think these numbers make the game more exciting? Why or why not?

_____

_____

_____

_____

_____

_____

_____

_____

_____

_____

_____

_____

_____

_____

_____

#50924—*180 Days of Reading for Third Grade* © *Shell Education*

NAME:_____ DATE:_____

DIRECTIONS Read the text and then answer the questions.

SCORE

Monica read an article. It was about a basketball star. Monica wanted to know his secret. How did he become an amazing athlete? She wants to improve, too. She is working on her skills in softball. She learned that the athlete worked hard. He was serious. He believed in himself. This helped Monica focus on her own strengths.

1. Ⓨ Ⓝ

2. Ⓨ Ⓝ

3. Ⓨ Ⓝ

1. What is this text about?

Ⓐ It is about rooting for an athlete.

Ⓑ It is about basketball players wearing glasses to see the ball.

Ⓒ It is about the importance of believing in yourself and working hard.

Ⓓ It is about watching a ball.

2. Who is the main character?

Ⓐ a basketball star

Ⓑ Monica

Ⓒ Monica's basketball team

Ⓓ Monica's softball team

3. What suffix could be added to the root word *work* to make a new word?

Ⓐ –es

Ⓑ –ly

Ⓒ –tion

Ⓓ –er

4. Ⓨ Ⓝ

5. Ⓨ Ⓝ

4. What is the definition of *focus*?

Ⓐ improve

Ⓑ pay close attention to

Ⓒ support

Ⓓ move quickly

___ / 5

Total

5. Which phrase is an example of alliteration?

Ⓐ knows his secret

Ⓑ the athlete worked hard

Ⓒ amazing athlete

Ⓓ focus on her own

NAME: _____ **DATE:** _____

SCORE

DIRECTIONS Read the text and then answer the questions.

1. Y N

2. Y N

   Josie and Kevin picked a movie. They had different opinions. Josie wanted a happy ending. Kevin wanted a lot of action. After the movie, they shared their ideas. They both liked it. Kevin wanted it to be more exciting. Josie wished the characters were happy in the end. It was still a good flick!

3. Y N

4. Y N

5. Y N

___ / 5
Total

1. Which title best fits this text?

  A Different Opinions

  B Bad Movie Endings

  C Happy or Action?

  D No Happiness

2. How could you describe the opinions of the two main characters?

  A Josie and Kevin cannot agree on which movie to watch.

  B Josie and Kevin agree on how the movie should have ended.

  C Josie and Kevin have different opinions, but they both hated the movie.

  D Josie and Kevin have different opinions, but they both liked the movie.

3. Which word is the root word in *shared*?

  A hare

  B share

  C hared

  D are

4. Which word means *a personal view*?

  A opinion

  B ending

  C happy

  D action

5. Which word is used to tell the reader that two things are being compared?

  A movie

  B wanted

  C both

  D end

 #50924—180 Days of Reading for Third Grade

NAME:_____ **DATE:**_____

DIRECTIONS   Read the text and then answer the questions.

"It's testing day today," the teacher reminds the students. "Remember that the test is timed. I will keep an eye on the clock. When the bell rings, the test will be over. You have forty-five minutes to answer the questions." The students begin by opening their test books and reading the directions. They don't want to hear the bell until they are finished!

1. Which picture would tell a reader more about this text?

Ⓐ a picture of a pencil

Ⓑ a picture of a student reading

Ⓒ a picture of a bell

Ⓓ a picture of a clock and a test

2. What is the setting?

Ⓐ a classroom

Ⓑ a bookstore

Ⓒ the playground

Ⓓ at home

3. Which word is the root word in *reading*?

Ⓐ read

Ⓑ reader

Ⓒ ding

Ⓓ ead

4. Which of these words mean the same thing?

Ⓐ *over* and *finish*

Ⓑ *hear* and *rings*

Ⓒ *bell* and *timed*

Ⓓ *answer* and *reading*

5. What is the tone of the last sentence?

Ⓐ hopeless

Ⓑ casual

Ⓒ nervous

Ⓓ thankful

1. Ⓨ Ⓝ

2. Ⓨ Ⓝ

3. Ⓨ Ⓝ

4. Ⓨ Ⓝ

5. Ⓨ Ⓝ

___ / 5
Total

NAME: _____ DATE: _____

Taking the Shot

I have always hated games that come down to the final seconds. I can't stand to watch them, and I can't stand to play in them. It makes me too anxious to know that anything can happen and that the end result could be a disappointment.

So you can imagine how it felt to have about one minute left on the clock during our soccer game last weekend. Our team was playing the Devils, and the score was 4–3. We were down by one goal and hoping to score before the final whistle. If we could tie the game, the two teams would play in overtime for a winner.

This was an important game. It was the last one of the season. The winner of this game would move on to the city championship. It was a very tense time.

I was playing the forward position on that day and was running the ball up the field with my friend, Alex. We were passing it back and forth and making a lot of progress. I could hear the crowd cheering and thought I even heard my mom yell my name. I was very focused, so all I could do was keep my eye on the ball and watch the goal. I was looking for any opening to make a shot. I knew the goalie was a bit slow, so if he had to run after a ball quickly, it might just slip past him. It was my only hope.

In an instant, I saw my chance. I could see a line straight through to the net. All I needed was a hard kick. I was sure that the ball would sail right past the goalie. I planted my left foot and aimed my right leg toward the goal. I kicked that ball with all my might. I watched the ball, almost as if it were in slow motion, go right into the goalie's hands. Then, I heard the whistle. The game was over, and we had lost. I have never felt such disappointment before. It did not matter that my coach gave me a high-five and told me I had a good game or that my teammates kept saying, "Nice try!" I wanted to win so badly, but I missed the shot.

NAME:_____ **DATE:**_____

DIRECTIONS Read "Taking the Shot" and then answer the questions.

1. Which statement is true about the narrator?

- Ⓐ He does not like close games.
- Ⓑ He is a horrible soccer player.
- Ⓒ He did not want to go to the city championship.
- Ⓓ He does not trust Alex.

2. What is the author's opinion?

- Ⓐ It is better to be a team player than to hog the ball.
- Ⓑ Losing a game is the worst thing to ever happen.
- Ⓒ Losing an important game can be very disappointing.
- Ⓓ Soccer is too competitive.

3. Who would most likely relate to the narrator's experience?

- Ⓐ a goalie who catches a ball
- Ⓑ a teacher who forgets to give a spelling test
- Ⓒ a chef who burns a meal and has to start over
- Ⓓ a gymnast who falls and causes her team to lose

4. Which summary of the text is most accurate?

- Ⓐ The narrator likes to play soccer with his friend, Alex.
- Ⓑ The narrator misses his doctor's appointment.
- Ⓒ The narrator makes a goal and wins the game.
- Ⓓ The narrator misses his chance to score a goal.

5. What is a theme of this text?

- Ⓐ Learning how to lose gracefully is important.
- Ⓑ Hard work can pay off.
- Ⓒ Team sports are only about winning and losing.
- Ⓓ A game can be saved by a whistle.

6. What other type of text is related to this text?

- Ⓐ a poem about soccer
- Ⓑ a nonfiction text about soccer rules
- Ⓒ a letter to the editor of a newspaper about keeping parks clean
- Ⓓ a fictional story about a swimmer who loses a race

1. Ⓨ Ⓝ

2. Ⓨ Ⓝ

3. Ⓨ Ⓝ

4. Ⓨ Ⓝ

5. Ⓨ Ⓝ

6. Ⓨ Ⓝ

___ / 6
Total

NAME: _____ **DATE:** _____

DIRECTIONS Reread "Taking the Shot." Then, read the prompt and respond on the lines below.

Think about how disappointed the narrator feels when he misses the goal in the soccer game. When have you felt disappointed by something that you did? How did you recover from that feeling?

_____

_____

_____

_____

_____

_____

_____

_____

_____

_____

_____

_____

_____

_____

_____

_____

#50924—180 Days of Reading for Third Grade   © Shell Education

NAME:_____ DATE:_____

DIRECTIONS Read the text and then answer the questions.

People around the world speak different languages. Each region has its own native language. Some people learn to speak more than one language. They may need one language to talk with family or friends. They may require another language for school or work. Learning to speak new languages can be a lot of fun!

1. Which word summarizes the topic of this text?

Ⓐ native

Ⓑ language

Ⓒ learning

Ⓓ people

2. In which chapter would this text belong?

Ⓐ Language Class

Ⓑ Speaking Two Languages

Ⓒ A Baby's First Word

Ⓓ Translating Troubles

3. Which word from the text could have an –ly added to make a new word?

Ⓐ learn

Ⓑ require

Ⓒ work

Ⓓ new

4. What is a synonym for the word *require*?

Ⓐ see

Ⓑ need

Ⓒ reach

Ⓓ involve

5. What does the phrase *native language* mean in the text?

Ⓐ the language of a child

Ⓑ the language of a specific place

Ⓒ the language of the wealthy

Ⓓ the language of nature

1. Ⓨ Ⓝ

2. Ⓨ Ⓝ

3. Ⓨ Ⓝ

4. Ⓨ Ⓝ

5. Ⓨ Ⓝ

___ / 5
Total

NAME:_____ DATE:_____

SCORE

1. (Y)(N)

2. (Y)(N)

3. (Y)(N)

4. (Y)(N)

5. (Y)(N)

___ / 5
Total

DIRECTIONS Read the text and then answer the questions.

Global warming is a serious problem. As the planet warms, glaciers melt. This causes the ocean waters to rise. Some towns are right on the coast. People who live in these coastal areas are nervous about the water levels. Their towns could be covered by water. Many people are doing what they can to reverse these changes.

1. Which phrase from the text tells a reader most about this text?

(A) glaciers melt

(B) right on the coast

(C) reverse these changes

(D) global warming is a serious problem

2. Which title best fits this text?

(A) Changing Glaciers

(B) Harm from Global Warming

(C) Heat Wave

(D) The Water Cycle

3. Which word has the same root word as *doing*?

(A) dong

(B) doable

(C) donut

(D) going

4. Which is **not** a synonym for *entire*?

(A) complete

(B) part

(C) whole

(D) full

5. What does the phrase *to reverse these changes* mean?

(A) fix a problem

(B) move backwards

(C) spin around

(D) give money

NAME:_____ DATE:_____

DIRECTIONS Read the text and then answer the questions.

A *natural preserve* is an area of land. It is set aside for wildlife. People cannot build or develop there. No hunting or fishing is allowed. Preserves are safe places for wildlife to live. They help species that are dying out. They protect endangered species.

1. (Y)(N)

2. (Y)(N)

3. (Y)(N)

1. Which is the best summary of the text?

(A) This text describes where natural preserves are located.

(B) This text describes why natural preserves are so important.

(C) This text describes why natural preserves do not work.

(D) This text describes why natural preserves are the same as national parks.

2. Which sample heading indicates the main idea?

(A) Wildlife Zone

(B) Endangered Species

(C) Protection at Natural Preserves

(D) Land Management

3. Which word has the same root word as *allowed*?

(A) wed

(B) disallow

(C) low

(D) lowly

4. Which is an antonym for the word *protect*?

(A) defend

(B) attack

(C) watch

(D) keep

5. What does the phrase *dying out* mean in this text?

(A) moving away

(B) becoming extinct

(C) dying quickly

(D) going outside

4. (Y)(N)

5. (Y)(N)

___ / 5
Total

NAME: _____ DATE: _____

Iceland

Iceland is a country in Europe. It is in a unique part of the world. Iceland is the most western country in Europe. It is surrounded by water. The capital is Reykjavik (REY-kyuh-veek).

The landscape of Iceland is remarkable. Part of the island is covered in glacial ice. Some of the coastline is created by *fjords* (fyohrdz). These are deep inlets. They are carved by glaciers.

Iceland is a volcanic island. There are many volcanoes there. There have been recent eruptions. The last big one was in 2010. It blew ash into the sky. Smoke made the air murky. It was hard for planes to fly around Europe.

Iceland

People in Iceland take care of their beautiful land. There are national parks. There are also many natural reserves. These areas are protected. The plants and animals are protected as well. This includes reindeer! Reindeer are found in Iceland.

The love of the land is shown in Iceland's flag. The flag includes three colors. There is red. This is a symbol of the island's volcanic fire. There is also white. This is a symbol of snow and ice. Finally, there is blue. This is a symbol for the ocean that surrounds the land.

Icelanders speak Icelandic. They also learn English. They are proud people. Iceland is quite small. It does not have a large amount of residents. The culture is shared with a small group of people. Yet it is a special place for many reasons.

NAME:_____ DATE:_____

DIRECTIONS Read "Iceland" and then answer the questions.

1. Which prediction is based on the title and image?

Ⓐ The text is about an icy land.

Ⓑ The text is about icy weather.

Ⓒ The text is about the country of Iceland.

Ⓓ The text is about mapping.

2. What is the author's purpose?

Ⓐ to share information about maps

Ⓑ to give opinions about life in Iceland

Ⓒ to persuade readers to love volcanoes

Ⓓ to share information about Iceland

3. Which statement shows prior knowledge related to the text?

Ⓐ I saw a reindeer in my Christmas book.

Ⓑ I have seen a picture of fjords in Iceland.

Ⓒ I am blonde and fair-skinned.

Ⓓ This text reminds me that my family speaks Spanish and English.

4. Which statement about the order of this text is true?

Ⓐ It is a sequential history of Iceland.

Ⓑ Each paragraph gives a different fact about Iceland.

Ⓒ The author compared and contrasted Iceland and Greenland.

Ⓓ The paragraphs are only about Iceland's landscape.

5. What is the main idea?

Ⓐ Iceland is a fascinating country with a unique landscape.

Ⓑ Iceland is a country in Europe.

Ⓒ Iceland has a flag with three colors.

Ⓓ Iceland is a small country with a small population.

6. Which detail describes the unique landscape?

Ⓐ The flag includes three colors.

Ⓑ Reindeer are found in Iceland.

Ⓒ Part of the island is covered in glacial ice.

Ⓓ Icelanders speak Icelandic.

1. ⓎⓃ

2. ⓎⓃ

3. ⓎⓃ

4. ⓎⓃ

5. ⓎⓃ

6. ⓎⓃ

___ / 6

Total

NAME:_____ DATE:_____

SCORE

___ / 4

DIRECTIONS Reread "Iceland." Then, read the prompt and respond on the lines below.

Think about the things that make Iceland unique and special. What connections can you make between Iceland and another place? What are the similarities between the two places?

_____

_____

_____

_____

_____

_____

_____

_____

_____

_____

_____

_____

_____

_____

_____

NAME: _____ **DATE:** _____

DIRECTIONS Read the text and then answer the questions.

Tim had to learn his multiplication facts, so his mom spent time with him each day working on his goal. He used flash cards and practiced really hard. He wanted to know his facts better than anyone else in his class, so he kept it up for weeks. After about two months, Tim took a timed test at school. He did very well, so his hard work had paid off!

1. ⓎⓃ

2. ⓎⓃ

3. ⓎⓃ

4. ⓎⓃ

5. ⓎⓃ

1. Which best summarizes the text?

Ⓐ Tim learns his multiplication facts.

Ⓑ Tim does well in school.

Ⓒ Hard work pays off.

Ⓓ Time studied for months.

2. How does the main character change from the beginning to the end of the text?

Ⓐ He forgets his multiplication facts after studying.

Ⓑ He studies for a test, so he does well on it.

Ⓒ He spends more time with his mother.

Ⓓ He becomes discouraged over his multiplication facts and fails his math test.

3. Which word from the text could have an *–ing* ending added to make a new word?

Ⓐ goal

Ⓑ work

Ⓒ paid

Ⓓ fact

4. Using context clues, what is the meaning of the word *goal* in the text?

Ⓐ score

Ⓑ the end of a race

Ⓒ something that someone wants to achieve

Ⓓ target area

5. What does the phrase *had paid off* mean?

Ⓐ cost a lot of money

Ⓑ was worth it and worked out well

Ⓒ was too exhausting

Ⓓ owed some change

____ / 5

Total

NAME: _____ DATE: _____

DIRECTIONS Read the text and then answer the questions.

1. Ⓨ Ⓝ

2. Ⓨ Ⓝ

3. Ⓨ Ⓝ

4. Ⓨ Ⓝ

5. Ⓨ Ⓝ

___ / 5
Total

My teacher says that math is all related. She says that addition and multiplication are similar. I do not see how that is possible. Then she uses pictures to show us. She shows us how to count groups together. Multiplication is about adding groups together. That makes a lot of sense. I will remember this when I have to solve math problems on my homework!

1. Which title best fits the text?

Ⓐ Counting Numbers

Ⓑ Groups

Ⓒ Multiplication Facts

Ⓓ Connections in Math

2. Who is the narrator?

Ⓐ a teacher

Ⓑ a parent

Ⓒ a student

Ⓓ a math expert

3. Which suffix can be added to *count* to make a new word?

Ⓐ –ly

Ⓑ –ed

Ⓒ –en

Ⓓ –ion

4. What is the definition of *solve* as it is used in this text?

Ⓐ find an answer to a math problem

Ⓑ unscramble

Ⓒ find an answer to a puzzle

Ⓓ deal with a problem

5. What other type of text is most similar to this text?

Ⓐ a gossip magazine

Ⓑ a newspaper

Ⓒ a textbook

Ⓓ a personal journal or diary

NAME: _____ **DATE:** _____

DIRECTIONS Read the text and then answer the questions.

Hannah was at the carnival with her family. She wanted to play the games with her dad. She really wanted to win a prize! Her dad tried hard, and finally, he was a winner! Hannah got to pick a prize, but she could not decide between the tall box or the flat box of candies. Her dad told her that the two boxes held the same amount. One had two rows of six, and the other had three rows of four. Both boxes had twelve candies!

1. Which statement shows a reader using the first sentence to accurately preview the text?

(A) This story is about a girl going to a carnival by herself.

(B) This story is about a girl in charge of a carnival.

(C) This story is about a girl going to a party with her family.

(D) This story is about a girl going to a carnival with her family.

2. Who are the two main characters?

(A) Hannah and her sister

(B) Hannah and her mom

(C) Hannah and her dad

(D) Hannah's mother and father

3. Which word from the text could have an *re–* prefix added to make a new word?

(A) family

(B) win

(C) fat

(D) play

4. Which is a synonym for the word *decide?*

(A) postpone

(B) determine

(C) accept

(D) rearrange

5. Which word is used to emphasize how much Hannah wanted to win a prize?

(A) really

(B) dad

(C) tall

(D) play

1. Ⓨ Ⓝ

2. Ⓨ Ⓝ

3. Ⓨ Ⓝ

4. Ⓨ Ⓝ

5. Ⓨ Ⓝ

___ / 5

Total

NAME:_____   DATE:_____

The Crayon Factory

The manager of a crayon factory had to design new crayon boxes. She had to choose how many crayons should go in each box. This also meant choosing how many rows were in each box. This was hard. She had to decide on four designs. Each design had to use the same number of crayons!

The factory crew gave the manager some ideas. They told her that they used multiplication to figure them out. They decided to start by having each box hold forty-eight crayons. Then, they figured out how forty-eight crayons would fit in boxes of different sizes.

First, Bob suggested a box with six rows. He said that there would be eight crayons in each row. The group checked Bob's work. They learned that his box would have forty-eight crayons. They kept his idea.

Next, Mei suggested a box with four rows. She said that there would be twelve crayons in each row. Some people did not believe that this would hold the same number of crayons as Bob's box. After doing the math, everyone realized that Mei's idea was correct, too.

Alberto decided to share his idea. He wanted to create a longer box for the crayons. He wanted only three rows for the box. He thought it would hold sixteen crayons in each row. The group liked this idea.

No one was sure if there were any other options. How else could they include forty-eight crayons? Sam had one more idea. He thought about it and realized that another longer box could hold two rows with twenty-four crayons in each row. Everyone agreed that this box may look odd, but it sure did hold forty-eight crayons.

The crew was proud of their ideas, and their manager was happy to have some feedback from others. Now they had to decide how to make these new types of boxes. At least the hard part was over!

NAME:_____ DATE:_____

DIRECTIONS Read "The Crayon Factory" and then answer the questions.

1. What could a reader learn from reading this text?

- Ⓐ Crayons are hard to make.
- Ⓑ Certain multiplication problems are equivalent.
- Ⓒ A factory crew works for a manager.
- Ⓓ Working on a team is not fun.

2. Why did the author include math in this text?

- Ⓐ to make the story funnier
- Ⓑ to compare multiplication to subtraction
- Ⓒ to explain a real problem at the local crayon factory
- Ⓓ to show how math relates to real life

3. Which statement shows a connection to the text?

- Ⓐ I added my markers, and I have 213.
- Ⓑ My dad works on a crew.
- Ⓒ This reminds me of making arrays for multiplication facts.
- Ⓓ I like red.

4. Which word best describes the crew that works at the factory?

- Ⓐ angry
- Ⓑ lazy
- Ⓒ cooperative
- Ⓓ mean

5. What important theme is shared in this text?

- Ⓐ A team working together can solve a lot of problems.
- Ⓑ A factory crew has to make big decisions.
- Ⓒ Crayons are very popular.
- Ⓓ Coworkers are not your friends.

6. Which well-known story is also about teamwork?

- Ⓐ "The Three Little Pigs"
- Ⓑ "The Frog Prince"
- Ⓒ "Cinderella"
- Ⓓ "Jack and the Beanstalk"

1. Ⓨ Ⓝ

2. Ⓨ Ⓝ

3. Ⓨ Ⓝ

4. Ⓨ Ⓝ

5. Ⓨ Ⓝ

6. Ⓨ Ⓝ

___ / 6
Total

NAME: _____ **DATE:** _____

DIRECTIONS Reread "The Crayon Factory." Then, read the prompt and respond on the lines below.

Think about how the workers at the crayon factory use math to help solve a problem. Explain in your own words how their solutions make sense. How do you know the math they used is correct?

_____

_____

_____

_____

_____

_____

_____

_____

_____

_____

_____

_____

_____

_____

_____

NAME:_____ DATE:_____

DIRECTIONS   Read the text and then answer the questions.

What is *metabolism* (muh-TAB-uh-liz-uhm)? It is how chemicals break down food. Food is turned into energy. Some animals can slow their metabolism. They do this when they hibernate. But animals do not need food while they rest. They do not use much energy.   A slower metabolism helps them conserve energy.

1. Ⓨ Ⓝ

2. Ⓨ Ⓝ

3. Ⓨ Ⓝ

1. Which word tells a reader most about this text?

Ⓐ animals

Ⓑ chemical

Ⓒ use

Ⓓ metabolism

4. What is the definition of *hibernate*?

Ⓐ energy

Ⓑ a deep sleep

Ⓒ a nap

Ⓓ metabolism

4. Ⓨ Ⓝ

5. Ⓨ Ⓝ

2. Which title best fits this text?

Ⓐ Slowing Down for Hibernation

Ⓑ Low Energy

Ⓒ Animal Diets

Ⓓ Diet Foods

5. Which word is defined within the text using a question?

Ⓐ metabolism

Ⓑ energy

Ⓒ chemicals

Ⓓ hibernate

___ / 5

Total

3. What prefix could you add to the root word *turn* to make a new word?

Ⓐ *un–*

Ⓑ *bi–*

Ⓒ *re–*

Ⓓ *dis–*

NAME: _____ **DATE:** _____

DIRECTIONS Read the text and then answer the questions.

1. Ⓨ Ⓝ

2. Ⓨ Ⓝ

3. Ⓨ Ⓝ

4. Ⓨ Ⓝ

5. Ⓨ Ⓝ

___ / 5
Total

Humans do not hibernate through the winter, like bears do. However, most people do conserve energy when they sleep. Humans have to adapt to the cold weather in winter, too. People usually spend more time indoors in the winter months. They may read, watch a movie, relax, or sit by the fire. When the weather is nice and warm, most people enjoy being outside.

1. Which heading best fits this text?

Ⓐ Relaxing by the Fire

Ⓑ Wintertime

Ⓒ Going Indoors

Ⓓ Do Humans Hibernate?

2. When do people conserve the most energy?

Ⓐ while eating

Ⓑ while watching movies

Ⓒ while sleeping

Ⓓ while reading

3. Which word from the text has a suffix?

Ⓐ outside

Ⓑ movie

Ⓒ usually

Ⓓ conserve

4. Which word is an antonym for *conserve*?

Ⓐ waste

Ⓑ eat

Ⓒ save

Ⓓ talk

5. What is the tone of this text?

Ⓐ informative

Ⓑ serious

Ⓒ funny

Ⓓ persuasive

NAME:_____ DATE:_____

DIRECTIONS Read the text and then answer the questions.

Bear attacks on humans are quite rare. Bears are shy and do not like to be around people. Some people do encounter bears in the wild. In some places, bears roam near humans in order to get food. People should keep a distance from bears. Bears with cubs are very protective and will attack if they sense danger. Making noise and backing away slowly are good things to do if you see a bear.

1. Which type of image would tell a reader more about this text?

- Ⓐ a picture of a human hiking
- Ⓑ a chart showing how rare bear attacks are
- Ⓒ a photograph of a campground
- Ⓓ a weather report

2. Which title best fits this text?

- Ⓐ Survival Techniques
- Ⓑ Roaming for Food
- Ⓒ Rare Bear Attacks
- Ⓓ Protecting Youngsters

3. Which word is the root word in *slowly*?

- Ⓐ lowly
- Ⓑ low
- Ⓒ slow
- Ⓓ ow

4. What is a synonym for *encounter*?

- Ⓐ smell
- Ⓑ hear
- Ⓒ meet
- Ⓓ feel

5. Which word describes the tone of this text?

- Ⓐ warning
- Ⓑ serious
- Ⓒ funny
- Ⓓ sad

1. Ⓨ Ⓝ

2. Ⓨ Ⓝ

3. Ⓨ Ⓝ

4. Ⓨ Ⓝ

5. Ⓨ Ⓝ

___ / 5

Total

NAME: _____ DATE: _____

Sleeping for Survival

Many animals take a long rest during the winter months. They are not napping. They are *hibernating*. This is like a very deep sleep. It helps animals survive. Animals cannot be active during this time; otherwise, they would need to find food. This is very hard to do in places it is snowy and icy. It also takes a lot of energy to stay warm. It is hard to create enough energy when you cannot find food.

An animal's body temperature drops while hibernating. Breathing slows down. Animals do not wake easily. They do not eat or make waste. They stay in a very deep sleep. How long they do this varies from animal to animal.

What kinds of animals hibernate? Bears are very efficient hibernators. Some bears can go for seven months! Chipmunks, raccoons, and skunks hibernate. Mice, bats, and hamsters do, too. These are a few of the animals that sleep through the winter.

Most people believe that animals only hibernate in the winter. Some animals actually hibernate in the summer. They are trying to escape hot and dry weather. They may also have to survive with little or no water. This is called *estivation*. One animal that rests in the summer is the frog. Certain species of frogs will bury themselves. They may do this in soil or under a log or a rock. Some find a dry pond to burrow into. Frogs are cold-blooded animals. They cannot stay warmer or cooler than their surroundings. When it is a very hot day, the frogs cannot keep cool enough to survive. Estivation helps them stay alive.

Both of these types of hibernation help animals survive. They adjust to their environment. They learn how to stay alive in harsh climates.

NAME:_____ DATE:_____

DIRECTIONS Read "Sleeping for Survival" and then answer the questions.

1. What is the purpose for reading this text?

- Ⓐ to be entertained
- Ⓑ to be persuaded to believe something
- Ⓒ to be informed about animals
- Ⓓ to be informed about hibernation

2. What does the author want to teach the reader in this text?

- Ⓐ that animals can die easily when hibernating
- Ⓑ that animals hibernate to be better predators
- Ⓒ that animals hibernate in the winter and the summer
- Ⓓ that some animals hibernate because all other animals do, too

3. Which statement reflects prior knowledge related to the text?

- Ⓐ I don't know the difference between chipmunks and squirrels.
- Ⓑ I have studied the hibernation patterns of bears.
- Ⓒ I have hiked in the forest in winter.
- Ⓓ I think frogs and toads are alike.

4. What topics were compared in this text?

- Ⓐ animals that hibernate and animals that don't hibernate
- Ⓑ animals that hibernate in the winter and animals that hibernate in the summer
- Ⓒ bears and chipmunks
- Ⓓ animals that hibernate and animals that nap

5. What is the most important idea in this text?

- Ⓐ Hibernation confuses animals.
- Ⓑ Hibernation harms animals.
- Ⓒ Hibernation helps animals survive.
- Ⓓ Hibernation calms animals down.

6. How does hibernation help animals survive?

- Ⓐ It lowers their metabolism.
- Ⓑ It keeps them from eating when food is scarce.
- Ⓒ It conserves their energy when it is cold or snowy.
- Ⓓ all of the above

1. Ⓨ Ⓝ

2. Ⓨ Ⓝ

3. Ⓨ Ⓝ

4. Ⓨ Ⓝ

5. Ⓨ Ⓝ

6. Ⓨ Ⓝ

___ / 6

Total

NAME: _____ **DATE:** _____

DIRECTIONS Reread "Sleeping for Survival." Then, read the prompt and respond on the lines below.

Think about why animals hibernate in the summer or the winter. What are the differences and similarities between animals that hibernate in the summer or winter?

_____

_____

_____

_____

_____

_____

_____

_____

_____

_____

_____

_____

_____

_____

_____

_____

#50924—180 Days of Reading for Third Grade   © Shell Education

NAME:_____ **DATE:**_____

DIRECTIONS Read the text and then answer the questions.

Stacy was learning about fables at school. She had never read one before. *Fables* are fictional stories. Fables might include animals or plants as characters. There might be pretend creatures. The characters act like humans. Fables have a *moral*, or a lesson. Stacy enjoyed reading this type of fantasy story—she loved the talking animals!

1. Ⓨ Ⓝ

2. Ⓨ Ⓝ

3. Ⓨ Ⓝ

1. Which title best fits this text?

Ⓐ Talking Animals

Ⓑ Fable Characters

Ⓒ Stacy's Favorites

Ⓓ Story Characters

4. What is the meaning of the word *pretend* in this text?

Ⓐ alien

Ⓑ live

Ⓒ make-believe

Ⓓ mean

4. Ⓨ Ⓝ

5. Ⓨ Ⓝ

2. Why did Stacy enjoy reading fables?

Ⓐ They have funny characters that act like humans.

Ⓑ They are fictional stories.

Ⓒ They are popular.

Ⓓ They have magic.

5. What does the language of this text tell you about Stacy?

Ⓐ She disliked school.

Ⓑ She was a silly girl.

Ⓒ She did not read much.

Ⓓ She was happy to learn about this new type of story.

___/5

Total

3. Which word includes the same *en–* prefix as *enjoyed*?

Ⓐ enemy

Ⓑ enact

Ⓒ end

Ⓓ energy

NAME:_____ DATE:_____

SCORE

1. Ⓨ Ⓝ

2. Ⓨ Ⓝ

3. Ⓨ Ⓝ

4. Ⓨ Ⓝ

5. Ⓨ Ⓝ

___ / 5
Total

DIRECTIONS Read the text and then answer the questions.

Lin was always trying to stay home from school. She liked staying home because she got to watch movies and rest. Many days, she complained that her stomach hurt. Her father let her stay home. After a while, her father realized Lin was not telling the truth. One day when she asked to stay home, her father said, "You have to go to school." Lin was very angry because her stomach really did hurt that day, but she had used that excuse too many times.

1. Which title best fits the text?

Ⓐ No More Excuses

Ⓑ Lin's Day Off

Ⓒ Stomach Ache

Ⓓ A Day at the Movies

2. Which story is similar to this text?

Ⓐ "Cinderella"

Ⓑ "The Boy Who Cried Wolf"

Ⓒ "Jack and the Beanstalk"

Ⓓ "Hansel and Gretel"

3. Which word has the same root word as *really*?

Ⓐ early

Ⓑ unreal

Ⓒ ally

Ⓓ tally

4. Where could a reader look to find synonyms for *complained*?

Ⓐ a thesaurus

Ⓑ an encyclopedia

Ⓒ an atlas

Ⓓ a dictionary

5. What does the phrase *used that excuse* mean?

Ⓐ said sorry

Ⓑ lied by claiming false reasons

Ⓒ screamed

Ⓓ left the house

NAME: _____ **DATE:** _____

DIRECTIONS Read the text and then answer the questions.

The farmer and his wife were worried about their crops. It had been a very dry winter and spring, and people assumed there would be a drought by summertime. This was bad news for the farmers in the area. It was not easy to plant seeds in hard, dry land. "If only we had tons of money in the bank," the farmer wished.

1. Which picture would tell a reader more about this text?

Ⓐ a picture of a wintery scene

Ⓑ a picture of wilting crops

Ⓒ a picture of a goose

Ⓓ a picture of a tractor

2. Which word best describes the main characters?

Ⓐ angry

Ⓑ concerned

Ⓒ confused

Ⓓ ecstatic

3. Which word includes the same root word as *wished*?

Ⓐ whisk

Ⓑ dish

Ⓒ wishes

Ⓓ washed

4. Where could a reader look to find the definition of *drought*?

Ⓐ a thesaurus

Ⓑ an encyclopedia

Ⓒ an atlas

Ⓓ a dictionary

5. Reread the last sentence. Which figure of speech does this sentence contain?

Ⓐ a simile

Ⓑ personification

Ⓒ alliteration

Ⓓ hyperbole

1. Ⓨ Ⓝ

2. Ⓨ Ⓝ

3. Ⓨ Ⓝ

4. Ⓨ Ⓝ

5. Ⓨ Ⓝ

___ / 5
Total

NAME: _____ DATE: _____

The Lion's Share

One day, a lion, a fox, a jackal, and a wolf went hunting together. They hunted all morning. But they could not find anything satisfactory. It was only in the late afternoon that they finally caught a deer. The four beasts surrounded the poor animal. They killed it as fast as they could. Then they decided to share their food.

The lion was the Lord of the Jungle. He was superior to all in strength. Hence, the other creatures agreed when he proposed to share the food for all. Placing one of his paws upon the deer, the lion said, "You see, as a member of the hunting party, it is my right to receive one of these portions."

The others nodded in agreement. "But I am also the King of Beasts. So I must receive another portion," he declared. The others looked uneasily at each other. "And besides, I was leading the hunt. So I deserve a third portion," he proclaimed.

The others mumbled something, but it could not be heard. "As for the fourth portion, if you wish to argue with me about its ownership, let's begin, and we will see who will get it."

"Humph," the others grumbled. They walked away with their heads down. They knew it was pointless to argue about their shares.

Moral: You may share the labors of the great, but you cannot share the spoils.

NAME:_____ DATE:_____

Read "The Lion's Share" and then answer the questions.

SCORE

1. Which purpose for reading this fable makes the most sense?

Ⓐ to learn the deer's perspective

Ⓑ to be entertained and learn a lesson at the end

Ⓒ to learn about hunting

Ⓓ to understand how animals act together in the wild

2. How many portions of food did the lion get?

Ⓐ one portion

Ⓑ two portions

Ⓒ three portions

Ⓓ all of the portions

3. Which statement shows a connection to the moral?

Ⓐ I saw a fox and a wolf at the zoo.

Ⓑ My pet dog and pet cat fight over who gets to lie under the table.

Ⓒ My older brother made me help him do his chores but did not give me any part of his allowance.

Ⓓ My parents do not let me eat as much dessert as they do.

4. Which word describes the lion's character?

Ⓐ friendly

Ⓑ untrustworthy

Ⓒ giving

Ⓓ uneasy

5. Which theme relates to the fox, jackal, and wolf?

Ⓐ Do not always trust your superiors.

Ⓑ No hunting after dark.

Ⓒ Killing other animals is wrong.

Ⓓ Working together will get you nowhere.

6. Which type of text is most closely related to "The Lion's Share"?

Ⓐ a fictional story that takes place on an African safari

Ⓑ a nonfiction text about protecting endangered species

Ⓒ a nonfiction text about the diet of lions

Ⓓ a fictional story about a friend who is the leader of a group and makes decisions for the other kids

1. Ⓨ Ⓝ

2. Ⓨ Ⓝ

3. Ⓨ Ⓝ

4. Ⓨ Ⓝ

5. Ⓨ Ⓝ

6. Ⓨ Ⓝ

___ / 6
Total

SCORE

___ / 4

NAME: _____ **DATE:** _____

DIRECTIONS Reread "The Lion's Share." Then, read the prompt and respond on the lines below.

Reread the moral of this fable. Does this lesson seem fair to you? Why or why not?

_____

_____

_____

_____

_____

_____

_____

_____

_____

_____

_____

_____

_____

_____

_____

NAME:_____ **DATE:**_____

DIRECTIONS Read the text and then answer the questions.

Sacajawea (sak-uh-juh-WEE-uh) played a big role in history. She was an American Indian. She made a trip with Lewis and Clark. Most people believe she joined because of her husband. He was a translator. He worked for the group. They needed help speaking with different tribes. Sacajawea helped, too. She knew the landscape. She could also speak to other American Indians. This helped the group make trades and find food.

1. Ⓨ Ⓝ

2. Ⓨ Ⓝ

3. Ⓨ Ⓝ

1. Who is this text about?

Ⓐ Lewis

Ⓑ Sacajawea

Ⓒ Clark

Ⓓ American Indians

2. Which title best describes the main idea?

Ⓐ The Sacrifice of Sacajawea

Ⓑ Sacajawea's Husband

Ⓒ Sacajawea's Contribution

Ⓓ Tribal Language

3. Which word could add the prefix *dis–* to make another word?

Ⓐ group

Ⓑ speak

Ⓒ believe

Ⓓ food

4. What is another form of the verb *speaking*?

Ⓐ speeding

Ⓑ talking

Ⓒ peak

Ⓓ spoke

4. Ⓨ Ⓝ

5. Ⓨ Ⓝ

5. Which word describes the tone of this text?

Ⓐ informative

Ⓑ silly

Ⓒ funny

Ⓓ false

___ / 5

Total

NAME:_____ DATE:_____

SCORE

1. Ⓨ Ⓝ

2. Ⓨ Ⓝ

3. Ⓨ Ⓝ

4. Ⓨ Ⓝ

5. Ⓨ Ⓝ

___ / 5
Total

DIRECTIONS Read the text and then answer the questions.

Lewis and Clark learned so much about the land in the region. They observed many new plants and animals. They gathered facts about these new species. They brought that information home with them. They wanted to share it with others. Lewis and Clark were the first to discover the magpie bird. They saw these birds in 1804.

1. Which statement shows a connection to the text?

Ⓐ Mrs. Lewis is my piano teacher.

Ⓑ I think pigeons are annoying.

Ⓒ I like to notice things in nature like Lewis and Clark did.

Ⓓ I want a new pet animal in my home.

2. Which chapter title best fits this text?

Ⓐ A Map of Lewis and Clark's Journey

Ⓑ Observations by Lewis and Clark

Ⓒ The End of an Expedition

Ⓓ Plants in the West

3. Which root word could add the prefix re– to make another word?

Ⓐ three

Ⓑ first

Ⓒ new

Ⓓ bird

4. Which word is a synonym for *gathered*?

Ⓐ compared

Ⓑ argued

Ⓒ noticed

Ⓓ collected

5. What does the language tell you about the author's purpose?

Ⓐ The language is personal so that people will feel like they know Lewis and Clark.

Ⓑ The language is factual so that people will learn more about Lewis and Clark.

Ⓒ The language is funny so that people will laugh about Lewis and Clark.

Ⓓ The language is persuasive so that people will believe things about Lewis and Clark.

NAME:_____ DATE:_____

DIRECTIONS Read the text and then answer the questions.

Thomas Jefferson was the third president. He had dreams of exploring the West. For years, he tried to find a way to organize a group to explore. Lewis and Clark were one group he sent to gather facts about the new land. He ordered other groups to other parts of the country. He wanted the country to extend to the West Coast. Many years later, that is what happened.

1. Ⓨ Ⓝ

2. Ⓨ Ⓝ

3. Ⓨ Ⓝ

4. Ⓨ Ⓝ

5. Ⓨ Ⓝ

___ / 5

Total

1. What type of visual would tell more about this text?

Ⓐ a picture of the White House

Ⓑ a map of the United States

Ⓒ a portrait of George Washington

Ⓓ a chart showing how much money Jefferson paid Lewis and Clark

2. Which index entry would help a reader find this information?

Ⓐ Jefferson at war

Ⓑ Jefferson's presidency

Ⓒ role of Jefferson in expedition

Ⓓ Jefferson's childhood

3. Which word is the root word in *exploring*?

Ⓐ ring

Ⓑ polar

Ⓒ explode

Ⓓ explore

4. Which of these words are synonyms?

Ⓐ *dreams* and *places*

Ⓑ *extend* and *stretch*

Ⓒ *organize* and *happened*

Ⓓ *ordered* and *sent*

5. What does the phrase *that is what happened* refer to?

Ⓐ Thomas Jefferson died.

Ⓑ The country extended to the West Coast.

Ⓒ Thomas Jefferson explored the West himself.

Ⓓ Thomas Jefferson met Lewis and Clark.

NAME:_____   DATE:_____

Lewis and Clark

More than 200 years ago, people did not know a lot about the western part of the United States. Going west was an exciting adventure. It was also a difficult journey.

Two famous explorers made that trip. They were named Meriwether Lewis and William Clark. They traveled when little was known about the West. There were no maps to tell them the way. Their goal was to reach the Pacific Ocean.

Lewis and Clark began their journey in 1804. It was not just two men doing all the work on this trip. They brought many people along to help. More than forty people joined Lewis and Clark. They packed a lot of food and supplies for the whole group.

Lewis and Clark kept good records of their journey. They both kept detailed records of where they went. Clark made maps of their journey. The maps showed the route they took as well as the rivers and mountains they crossed. Lewis kept notes in a journal about the journey and the places they stayed. He also recorded information about plants and animals they saw along the way.

Many American Indians helped Lewis and Clark during their trip. They worked as guides to show the explorers where to go. They also helped the group find food and other supplies.

Lewis and Clark finally reached the ocean shore. They had been traveling for more than a year. They were thrilled to see the Pacific Ocean. They were also eager to go home. The group knew they had another long trip to return to Missouri. They spent the winter at an area they called Fort Clatsop. Today, this area is in the state of Oregon. After about six months, they began the journey home.

map of the Lewis and Clark expedition

Lewis and Clark taught people about the new land in the West. Their stories and maps were very helpful for people who traveled after their journey. Today, the trip that used to take an entire year would take a few hours on an airplane. A lot has changed since the time of Lewis and Clark.

NAME: _____ **DATE:** _____

> **DIRECTIONS** Read "Lewis and Clark" and then answer the questions.

1. Which summary is the most accurate for the text?

Ⓐ This is about explorers named Lewis and Clark.

Ⓑ This is about brothers named Lewis and Clark.

Ⓒ This is about a store named Lewis and Clark.

Ⓓ This is about a town named Lewis and Clark.

2. What is the author's purpose?

Ⓐ to teach people about geography

Ⓑ to inform people about Lewis and Clark

Ⓒ to make people enjoy and laugh at this text

Ⓓ to teach people about American Indians

3. Which statement shows a connection to the text?

Ⓐ I do not like to go on boats.

Ⓑ I have always wanted to explore the world and see new places.

Ⓒ I know there are seven oceans.

Ⓓ I live in the state of Texas.

4. How is the text organized?

Ⓐ It is sequential, explaining every single step that they took.

Ⓑ It is chronological, explaining from start to finish.

Ⓒ It compares Lewis and Clark to other explorers.

Ⓓ It describes how Lewis and Clark solved their problems.

5. What is the most important idea about Lewis and Clark?

Ⓐ They learned about the West and shared information with others.

Ⓑ They traveled slowly.

Ⓒ They traveled in three boats.

Ⓓ They wanted to reach the Pacific Ocean.

6. What did Lewis and Clark share about their trip?

Ⓐ how to navigate a boat

Ⓑ ways to survive the trip in the winter

Ⓒ facts about the new land in the West

Ⓓ how to survive the heat of the summer months

1. Ⓨ Ⓝ

2. Ⓨ Ⓝ

3. Ⓨ Ⓝ

4. Ⓨ Ⓝ

5. Ⓨ Ⓝ

6. Ⓨ Ⓝ

___ / 6
Total

NAME:_____ DATE:_____

DIRECTIONS Reread "Lewis and Clark." Then, read the prompt and respond on the lines below.

Think about what it must have been like for Lewis and Clark to go somewhere for the first time. When have you done something for the first time? How did you feel doing it?

_____

_____

_____

_____

_____

_____

_____

_____

_____

_____

_____

_____

_____

_____

NAME:_____ **DATE:**_____

| DIRECTIONS | Read the text and then answer the questions. |

   The raccoon was acting very suspiciously. The other animals noticed. Finally, the cat asked, "Where were you last night?" The raccoon did not say anything. He did not want the others to know about his secret hiding place. All the goodies he found around town were stashed there. He wondered how long he could keep it all hidden.

1. Which word tells the reader about the main character's behavior?

- (A) goodies
- (B) suspiciously
- (C) raccoon
- (D) hidden

2. Who is the main character?

- (A) the cat
- (B) the raccoon
- (C) the goodies
- (D) the secret hiding place

3. To which root word can you add the prefix *re–* to make a new word?

- (A) say
- (B) place
- (C) long
- (D) found

4. What do you think the word *goodies* means in the text?

- (A) special treats or items
- (B) trash
- (C) animals
- (D) friends

5. The language used in this text suggests that it comes from

- (A) a history book.
- (B) a fable.
- (C) a nonfiction text.
- (D) a picture book about animals.

1. (Y)(N)

2. (Y)(N)

3. (Y)(N)

4. (Y)(N)

5. (Y)(N)

___/5
Total

NAME:_____ DATE:_____

SCORE

1. Ⓨ Ⓝ

2. Ⓨ Ⓝ

3. Ⓨ Ⓝ

4. Ⓨ Ⓝ

5. Ⓨ Ⓝ

___ / 5
Total

DIRECTIONS Read the text and then answer the questions.

The fox was tired of having such a bad reputation. All of the creatures in the forest were afraid of him. They avoided walking by him each day because they feared he would eat them. The truth was that the fox was lonely and he did not want to eat his forest friends anymore. He just wanted someone to talk to each day. He was sorry for all his bad deeds.

1. Which title best fits this text?

Ⓐ Lonely Guy

Ⓑ A New and Improved Fox

Ⓒ Bad Deeds

Ⓓ Moving Forward

2. What is the setting?

Ⓐ school

Ⓑ a castle

Ⓒ the forest

Ⓓ the beach

3. Which word is the root word in *wanted*?

Ⓐ wan

Ⓑ ant

Ⓒ want

Ⓓ ted

4. Who else would likely have a *bad reputation*?

Ⓐ a favorite teacher

Ⓑ a mom who gives her kids a special dessert

Ⓒ a police officer trying to keep kids safe

Ⓓ a bully who is always mean to other kids

5. What does the phrase *bad deeds* mean in the text?

Ⓐ angry voice

Ⓑ mistakes and poor behavior

Ⓒ kindness

Ⓓ habits

NAME:_____ DATE:_____

DIRECTIONS Read the text and then answer the questions.

Three little pigs got together. "Maybe we should build a house together," they said. They talked about materials and decided to make a wood house. The pigs felt that wood might be the most secure. The three little pigs worked together. They built a bedroom for each one of them. Teamwork helped them complete a successful project.

1. Y N

2. Y N

3. Y N

1. Which picture would tell a reader more about this text?

Ⓐ a picture of three beds

Ⓑ a picture of a building

Ⓒ a picture of tools

Ⓓ a picture of wood

4. Which of these words means *secure*?

Ⓐ colorful

Ⓑ stable

Ⓒ warm

Ⓓ open

4. Y N

5. Y N

2. Which word describes the main characters?

Ⓐ sad

Ⓑ cooperative

Ⓒ disagreeable

Ⓓ confused

5. Which genre is this text?

Ⓐ nonfiction

Ⓑ fiction

Ⓒ historical fiction

Ⓓ expository

___/5

Total

3. Which word has the same root word as *decided*?

Ⓐ side

Ⓑ decision

Ⓒ decade

Ⓓ decorate

NAME: _____ DATE: _____

The Hare's Bride:
A Brothers Grimm Tale

There was once a woman and her daughter who lived in a pretty garden with cabbages. A little hare came into it and ate all the cabbages during the wintertime. The mother told her daughter to shoo the hare away. The girl went into the garden. The little hare said, "Come, maiden. Come with me into my little hare's hut." The girl would not do it.

The next day, the hare came again and ate the cabbages. The mother told her daughter to shoo the hare away. The girl went into the garden. The little hare said, "Come, maiden. Come with me into my little hare's hut." The girl refused.

The third day the hare came again, and ate the cabbages. The mother told her daughter to shoo the hare away. The girl went into the garden. The little hare said, "Come, maiden. Come with me into my little hare's hut."

The girl sat on the little hare's tail. Then the hare took her far away to his little hut. He said, "Now, cook us green cabbage and millet-seed. I will invite the guests to our wedding."

Then all the wedding guests came. The girl was sad, for she was all alone in the kitchen. The little hare came back and said, "The wedding guests are hungry." The girl said nothing, and wept. The little hare went away. The little hare came back and said, "The wedding guests are waiting."

The girl said nothing, and the hare went away. Then the girl dressed a straw doll in her clothes and gave her a spoon and set her by the pan with the millet-seed and went back to her mother. The little hare came once more and said, "Serve the food!" and got up and touched the doll on the head so that her cap fell off. Then, the little hare saw that it was not his bride and was sad.

NAME:_____ DATE:_____

DIRECTIONS Read "The Hare's Bride: A Brothers Grimm Tale" and then answer the questions.

1. Which prediction was changed midway through reading this text?

(A) I predicted this was about two hares getting married, but now I realize it is a hare and a girl.

(B) I predicted this was about life in the forest, but now I know it takes place in a zoo.

(C) I predicted this was about two hares getting married, but now I think it is about a hare and a fox.

(D) I predicted this was a story about two hares being friends, but now I realize it is a hare's wedding.

2. What is one setting in the text?

(A) a cottage

(B) the cabbage garden

(C) the village market

(D) a wedding chapel

3. Who would be most similar to the hare?

(A) a dog who loves his master

(B) a fox who outsmarts a farmer

(C) a cat who sleeps all day

(D) a horse who saves a princess

4. How are the hare and the girl similar?

(A) They both trick each other.

(B) They both want to get married.

(C) They both love the daughter's mother.

(D) They both want to live in the hut.

5. What is the theme of this tale?

(A) You cannot always trust someone's words.

(B) Talking animals are scary.

(C) Weddings are always a special occasion.

(D) Hares are mean.

6. What other fairy tale has a similar theme?

(A) "Little Red Riding Hood"

(B) "Hansel and Gretel"

(C) "The Three Little Pigs"

(D) All of these tales are about characters tricking someone else.

1. (Y)(N)

2. (Y)(N)

3. (Y)(N)

4. (Y)(N)

5. (Y)(N)

6. (Y)(N)

___ / 6

Total

NAME:_____ DATE:_____

DIRECTIONS Reread "The Hare's Bride: A Brothers Grimm Tale." Then, read the prompt and respond on the lines below.

This story is about a very tricky hare who was tricked himself in the end. When have you tried to trick someone? Did your plan work?

_____

_____

_____

_____

_____

_____

_____

_____

_____

_____

_____

_____

_____

_____

#50924—180 Days of Reading for Third Grade

NAME: _____ **DATE:** _____

DIRECTIONS Read the text and then answer the questions.

The airplane is an amazing invention. Two brothers flew an airplane first. Orville and Wilbur Wright were the inventors. The Wright brothers studied flight for many years. They began their work with kites. They learned a lot about how kites fly. They flew an airplane for the first time in 1903.

1. Ⓨ Ⓝ

2. Ⓨ Ⓝ

1. Which summary of the text is most accurate?

Ⓐ This text is about different kinds of inventions.

Ⓑ This text is about different methods of transportation.

Ⓒ This text is about space.

Ⓓ This text is about how the airplane was invented.

2. Which index entry would direct a reader to this text?

Ⓐ Wright, Orville and Wilbur

Ⓑ different kinds of airplanes

Ⓒ airports

Ⓓ the physics of flights

3. Which suffix could replace –ed in *learned* to make a new word?

Ⓐ –er

Ⓑ –ly

Ⓒ –tion

Ⓓ –ment

4. What does *inventor* mean in this text?

Ⓐ an airplane

Ⓑ a creator of new things

Ⓒ amazing

Ⓓ a person who studies

5. What is an example of an *amazing invention* in today's world?

Ⓐ pencil

Ⓑ bread

Ⓒ cell phone

Ⓓ clothing

3. Ⓨ Ⓝ

4. Ⓨ Ⓝ

5. Ⓨ Ⓝ

___ / 5
Total

NAME:_____ DATE:_____

SCORE

1. Ⓨ Ⓝ

2. Ⓨ Ⓝ

3. Ⓨ Ⓝ

4. Ⓨ Ⓝ

5. Ⓨ Ⓝ

___ / 5
Total

DIRECTIONS Read the text and then answer the questions.

The Atlantic Ocean is the second-largest ocean. Flights cross this ocean each day. They are called *transatlantic flights*. Early pilots had to figure out how to cross this large body of water. Engines could not travel far enough to cross it. The first planes could not hold enough fuel, either. Today, long flights across the Atlantic are very common. That is a big change from the past.

1. Which word tells a reader most about the topic of this text?

Ⓐ pilot

Ⓑ transatlantic

Ⓒ travel

Ⓓ water

2. Which chapter title indicates the main idea?

Ⓐ The World's Oceans

Ⓑ Body of Water

Ⓒ Crossing the Atlantic

Ⓓ Making Waves

3. Which suffix could replace *–est* in *largest* to make a new word?

Ⓐ –ion

Ⓑ –ing

Ⓒ –ed

Ⓓ –er

4. Which definition of the word *cross* is used in this text?

Ⓐ angry

Ⓑ a figure of two lines perpendicular to each other

Ⓒ to go across or over

Ⓓ mixture

5. What does it mean that transatlantic flights are *very common*?

Ⓐ They are safe.

Ⓑ They happen often.

Ⓒ They are organized.

Ⓓ They fly in circles.

NAME:_____ **DATE:**_____

DIRECTIONS Read the text and then answer the questions.

   Altitude is an important part of flying. It refers to the height that the plane in the air is from the ground. There are rules for how high or low a plane can fly in the air. These rules are for safety. Instruments on the plane let the pilot know about altitude. An *altimeter* is one of the tools in a plane that measures altitude.

1. Ⓨ Ⓝ

2. Ⓨ Ⓝ

3. Ⓨ Ⓝ

1. Which statement shows a reader using the first sentence to accurately preview the text?

Ⓐ I think this text is about bird's flight.

Ⓑ I think this text is about landing and taking off in an airplane.

Ⓒ I think this text is about the flight level of airplanes.

Ⓓ I think this text is about the altitude of a tall mountain.

2. Which heading indicates the main idea of this text?

Ⓐ An Airplane's Flight Level

Ⓑ Pilot Training

Ⓒ High and Low

Ⓓ Reading Instruments

3. Which word has the same suffix as *flying*?

Ⓐ ring

Ⓑ trying

Ⓒ fling

Ⓓ lie

4. Ⓨ Ⓝ

5. Ⓨ Ⓝ

4. Which sentence uses *instruments* in the same way as this text?

Ⓐ The orchestra members warmed up their *instruments*.

Ⓑ Tests are *instruments* for monitoring students.

Ⓒ *Instruments* in a car measure speed.

Ⓓ The doctor used an *instrument* during his exam.

___ / 5

Total

5. Which words from the text are synonyms?

Ⓐ *instrument* and *tool*

Ⓑ *part* and *air*

Ⓒ *safety* and *off*

Ⓓ *ground* and *low*

NAME: _____ DATE: _____

The Life of Amelia Earhart

Amelia Earhart was interested in flying planes from a very young age. She was born in 1897 in Kansas. Amelia was quite a tomboy. She loved to climb trees. She hunted rats with a rifle. During these years, the use of airplanes became more common. Amelia took her first flight in 1920. She was hooked. The ride changed her life, and she knew her mission in life.

Earhart took her first flying lesson in 1921. She worked hard to save money. She was a nurse's aide. Then she worked as a social worker. All of her income went into savings. Soon, she had enough money to buy her first plane.

Earhart's first plane was bright yellow. She called it *Canary*. Earhart learned a lot about flying in that plane. She flew to an altitude of 14,000 feet. That was a record at that time. Her next record was being the first woman to fly across the Atlantic Ocean. She joined two other pilots as their passenger. Together they made the flight in about 21 hours.

Earhart set her sights on the next record. This time, she wanted to fly the Atlantic alone. She wanted to do a *solo* flight. Amelia's husband helped her plan the trip. He wanted to help her reach her goal. She planned to fly from Newfoundland to Paris in 1932. Bad weather forced her to land in Ireland. It was still a victory for Amelia. She showed the world that men and women could both fly solo safely across the Atlantic.

Amelia Earhart set out to tackle another challenge. She wanted to be the first woman to fly around the world. She left from Miami on June 1, 1937. She traveled over 20,000 miles. It was the final days of the trip. It was July 2. The weather was cloudy and wet. She took off from New Guinea. Amelia had a hard time hearing messages through her radio. She reported that she was "running north and south." Then the line was silent. Those were the last words anyone ever heard from Amelia. Experts are still trying to solve the mystery of what happened to Amelia and her airplane. Her bravery was inspiring. She showed the world that strong women can do great things!

Amelia Earhart

NAME:_____ **DATE:**_____

DIRECTIONS Read "The Life of Amelia Earhart" and then answer the questions.

SCORE

1. What is the main reason for reading a biography?

(A) to learn about history

(B) to compare the lives of famous people

(C) to learn about a person's life story

(D) to learn about a person's family

2. Which phrase from the text indicates the author's point of view about Earhart?

(A) *quite a tomboy*

(B) *bravery was inspiring*

(C) *social worker*

(D) *save money*

3. Which statement shows how prior knowledge can help understand the text?

(A) I have been to Miami on a vacation.

(B) I once took an airplane trip to my grandmother's house.

(C) I tried out for the boy's soccer team because my school does not have a girls' soccer team, and I wanted to prove that girls can play soccer just as well.

(D) My doctor has a nurse and a nurse's aide.

4. How is this biography organized?

(A) as a compare-and-contrast text

(B) chronologically, in the order that events happened

(C) sequentially, as the ordered steps to do something

(D) as a problem-and-solution text

5. What is the main lesson about Amelia Earhart's life?

(A) She flew better than anyone else.

(B) She took chances, was very brave, and taught people about equality among men and women.

(C) She liked to beat records.

(D) It is not known if she is dead or alive.

6. What is one way in which Amelia Earhart took chances?

(A) by climbing trees

(B) by learning to fly a plane

(C) by learning to fly a plane solo

(D) all of the above

1. (Y)(N)

2. (Y)(N)

3. (Y)(N)

4. (Y)(N)

5. (Y)(N)

6. (Y)(N)

___ / 6

Total

NAME:_____ **DATE:**_____

SCORE

___ / 4

DIRECTIONS Reread "The Life of Amelia Earhart." Then, read the prompt and respond on the lines below.

Think about the ways that Amelia was brave and courageous. Write about a time that you did something brave.

_____

_____

_____

_____

_____

_____

_____

_____

_____

_____

_____

_____

_____

_____

_____

ANSWER KEY

Week 1

Day 1
1. B
2. D
3. C
4. B
5. A

Day 2
1. B
2. B
3. B
4. C
5. B

Day 3
1. B
2. C
3. B
4. C
5. D

Day 4
1. B
2. C
3. C
4. D
5. A
6. D

Day 5
Responses will vary.

Week 2

Day 1
1. B
2. A
3. B
4. B
5. B

Day 2
1. A
2. B
3. A
4. B
5. D

Day 3
1. C
2. B
3. B
4. A
5. D

Day 4
1. C
2. C
3. B
4. C
5. C
6. B

Day 5
Responses will vary.

Week 3

Day 1
1. B
2. B
3. C
4. B
5. C

Day 2
1. B
2. B
3. C
4. B
5. C

Day 3
1. B
2. D
3. B
4. A
5. C

Day 4
1. A
2. D
3. C
4. B
5. C
6. C

Day 5
Responses will vary.

Week 4

Day 1
1. D
2. B
3. A
4. D
5. B

Day 2
1. C
2. B
3. A
4. C
5. A

Day 3
1. B
2. B
3. B
4. A
5. A

Day 4
1. C
2. C
3. A
4. A
5. A
6. C

Day 5
Responses will vary.

Week 5

Day 1
1. C
2. B
3. A
4. C
5. C

Day 2
1. B
2. B
3. B
4. C
5. D

Day 3
1. C
2. B
3. A
4. D
5. B

Day 4
1. C
2. B
3. C
4. C
5. D
6. D

Day 5
Responses will vary.

Week 6

Day 1
1. A
2. C
3. D
4. C
5. A

Day 2
1. A
2. B
3. C
4. B
5. A

Day 3
1. C
2. C
3. B
4. A
5. A

ANSWER KEY *(cont.)*

Week 6 *(cont.)*

Day 4
1. A
2. D
3. B
4. B
5. B
6. D

Day 5
  Responses will vary.

Week 7

Day 1
1. C
2. B
3. C
4. C
5. D

Day 2
1. A
2. B
3. B
4. B
5. B

Day 3
1. A
2. D
3. D
4. B
5. C

Day 4
1. B
2. C
3. B
4. A
5. B
6. C

Day 5
  Responses will vary.

Week 8

Day 1
1. C
2. B
3. B
4. C
5. A

Day 2
1. B
2. B
3. B
4. D
5. D

Day 3
1. C
2. B
3. D
4. B
5. A

Day 4
1. C
2. B
3. C
4. C
5. C
6. D

Day 5
  Responses will vary.

Week 9

Day 1
1. B
2. B
3. D
4. C
5. C

Day 2
1. A
2. B
3. B
4. D
5. C

Day 3
1. D
2. D
3. D
4. B
5. C

Day 4
1. C
2. C
3. A
4. D
5. B
6. A

Day 5
  Responses will vary.

Week 10

Day 1
1. B
2. B
3. A
4. A
5. A

Day 2
1. A
2. C
3. C
4. B
5. A

Day 3
1. C
2. A
3. D
4. B
5. D

Day 4
1. A
2. B
3. D
4. B
5. B
6. D

Day 5
  Responses will vary.

Week 11

Day 1
1. B
2. D
3. D
4. A
5. D

Day 2
1. C
2. C
3. A
4. D
5. B

Day 3
1. A
2. B
3. D
4. C
5. B

Day 4
1. B
2. B
3. B
4. B
5. B
6. C

Day 5
  Responses will vary.

Week 12

Day 1
1. D
2. C
3. B
4. D
5. A

ANSWER KEY *(cont.)*

Week 12 *(cont.)*

Day 2
1. A
2. D
3. C
4. C
5. D

Day 3
1. B
2. D
3. A
4. B
5. A

Day 4
1. C
2. D
3. D
4. A
5. A
6. B

Day 5
Responses will vary.

Week 13

Day 1
1. B
2. C
3. C
4. B
5. B

Day 2
1. A
2. C
3. A
4. B
5. C

Day 3
1. C
2. B
3. B
4. A
5. C

Day 4
1. B
2. C
3. C
4. D
5. D
6. C

Day 5
Responses will vary.

Week 14

Day 1
1. B
2. B
3. D
4. C
5. C

Day 2
1. D
2. C
3. C
4. B
5. B

Day 3
1. C
2. C
3. A
4. B
5. B

Day 4
1. B
2. C
3. D
4. D
5. B
6. C

Day 5
Responses will vary.

Week 15

Day 1
1. C
2. D
3. B
4. B
5. D

Day 2
1. B
2. D
3. B
4. B
5. B

Day 3
1. A
2. B
3. B
4. D
5. B

Day 4
1. B
2. B
3. C
4. B
5. A
6. B

Day 5
Responses will vary.

Week 16

Day 1
1. A
2. B
3. B
4. C
5. A

Day 2
1. B
2. B
3. C
4. D
5. D

Day 3
1. C
2. D
3. B
4. A
5. A

Day 4
1. B
2. C
3. B
4. A
5. A
6. B

Day 5
Responses will vary.

Week 17

Day 1
1. B
2. D
3. C
4. B
5. C

Day 2
1. B
2. A
3. B
4. C
5. C

Day 3
1. A
2. B
3. B
4. B
5. D

Day 4
1. C
2. A
3. B
4. C
5. A
6. A

ANSWER KEY *(cont.)*

Week 17 *(cont.)*

Day 5
Responses will vary.

Week 18

Day 1
1. C
2. B
3. A
4. C
5. A

Day 2
1. B
2. B
3. C
4. B
5. B

Day 3
1. A
2. C
3. C
4. B
5. A

Day 4
1. C
2. B
3. B
4. A
5. A
6. C

Day 5
Responses will vary.

Week 19

Day 1
1. B
2. A
3. C
4. C
5. C

Day 2
1. B
2. C
3. C
4. B
5. B

Day 3
1. A
2. B
3. D
4. B
5. B

Day 4
1. C
2. B
3. D
4. B
5. C
6. D

Day 5
Responses will vary.

Week 20

Day 1
1. B
2. C
3. B
4. C
5. C

Day 2
1. B
2. C
3. C
4. B
5. A

Day 3
1. D
2. C
3. B
4. D
5. A

Day 4
1. B
2. B
3. C
4. D
5. A
6. C

Day 5
Responses will vary.

Week 21

Day 1
1. D
2. A
3. C
4. B
5. D

Day 2
1. B
2. A
3. A
4. C
5. B

Day 3
1. C
2. C
3. A
4. D
5. C

Day 4
1. C
2. B
3. B
4. D
5. D
6. A

Day 5
Responses will vary.

Week 22

Day 1
1. D
2. C
3. D
4. B
5. A

Day 2
1. A
2. C
3. C
4. B
5. D

Day 3
1. D
2. B
3. A
4. B
5. D

Day 4
1. D
2. B
3. C
4. B
5. B
6. B

Day 5
Responses will vary.

Week 23

Day 1
1. B
2. D
3. B
4. D
5. C

Day 2
1. B
2. B
3. D
4. A
5. B

ANSWER KEY *(cont.)*

Week 23 *(cont.)*

Day 3
1. A
2. C
3. C
4. B
5. A

Day 4
1. B
2. B
3. D
4. A
5. A
6. C

Day 5
Responses will vary.

Week 24

Day 1
1. A
2. B
3. C
4. B
5. A

Day 2
1. A
2. D
3. B
4. A
5. B

Day 3
1. A
2. B
3. D
4. D
5. D

Day 4
1. B
2. D
3. C
4. C
5. A
6. B

Day 5
Responses will vary.

Week 25

Day 1
1. B
2. C
3. C
4. B
5. A

Day 2
1. A
2. A
3. B
4. C
5. B

Day 3
1. A
2. B
3. B
4. D
5. B

Day 4
1. C
2. A
3. B
4. D
5. D
6. C

Day 5
Responses will vary.

Week 26

Day 1
1. B
2. B
3. A
4. C
5. A

Day 2
1. C
2. D
3. B
4. C
5. D

Day 3
1. C
2. B
3. B
4. B
5. B

Day 4
1. C
2. A
3. B
4. C
5. B
6. C

Day 5
Responses will vary.

Week 27

Day 1
1. A
2. B
3. D
4. B
5. B

Day 2
1. B
2. A
3. D
4. B
5. B

Day 3
1. B
2. B
3. B
4. A
5. B

Day 4
1. B
2. A
3. B
4. B
5. B
6. C

Day 5
Responses will vary.

Week 28

Day 1
1. B
2. D
3. A
4. C
5. C

Day 2
1. B
2. B
3. C
4. B
5. D

Day 3
1. A
2. B
3. A
4. B
5. D

Day 4
1. A
2. B
3. B
4. C
5. B
6. B

Day 5
Responses will vary.

ANSWER KEY *(cont.)*

Week 29

Day 1
1. C
2. B
3. D
4. B
5. C

Day 2
1. A
2. D
3. B
4. A
5. C

Day 3
1. D
2. A
3. A
4. A
5. C

Day 4
1. A
2. C
3. D
4. D
5. A
6. D

Day 5
Responses will vary.

Week 30

Day 1
1. B
2. B
3. D
4. B
5. B

Day 2
1. D
2. B
3. B
4. B
5. A

Day 3
1. B
2. C
3. B
4. B
5. B

Day 4
1. C
2. D
3. B
4. B
5. A
6. C

Day 5
Responses will vary.

Week 31

Day 1
1. A
2. B
3. B
4. C
5. B

Day 2
1. D
2. C
3. B
4. A
5. D

Day 3
1. D
2. C
3. D
4. B
5. A

Day 4
1. B
2. D
3. C
4. C
5. A
6. A

Day 5
Responses will vary.

Week 32

Day 1
1. D
2. A
3. C
4. B
5. A

Day 2
1. D
2. C
3. C
4. A
5. A

Day 3
1. B
2. C
3. C
4. C
5. A

Day 4
1. D
2. C
3. B
4. B
5. C
6. D

Day 5
Responses will vary.

Week 33

Day 1
1. B
2. A
3. B
4. C
5. D

Day 2
1. A
2. B
3. B
4. A
5. B

Day 3
1. B
2. B
3. C
4. D
5. D

Day 4
1. B
2. D
3. C
4. B
5. A
6. D

Day 5
Responses will vary.

Week 34

Day 1
1. B
2. C
3. C
4. D
5. A

Day 2
1. C
2. B
3. C
4. D
5. B

Day 3
1. B
2. C
3. D
4. B
5. B

ANSWER KEY (cont.)

Week 34 (cont.)

Day 4
1. A
2. B
3. B
4. B
5. A
6. C

Day 5
Responses will vary.

Week 35

Day 1
1. B
2. B
3. B
4. A
5. B

Day 2
1. B
2. C
3. C
4. D
5. B

Day 3
1. D
2. B
3. B
4. B
5. B

Day 4
1. A
2. B
3. B
4. A
5. A
6. D

Day 5
Responses will vary.

Week 36

Day 1
1. D
2. A
3. A
4. B
5. C

Day 2
1. B
2. C
3. D
4. C
5. B

Day 3
1. C
2. A
3. B
4. C
5. A

Day 4
1. C
2. B
3. C
4. B
5. B
6. D

Day 5
Responses will vary.

REFERENCES CITED

Marzano, Robert. 2010. When Practice Makes Perfect…Sense. *Educational Leadership* 68 (3): 81–83.

National Reading Panel. 2000. Report of the National Reading Panel. *Teaching Children to Read: An Evidence-Based Assessment of the Scientific Research Literature on Reading and its Implication for Reading Instruction* (NIH Publication No. 00-4769). Washington, DC: U.S. Government Printing Office.

Rasinski, Timothy V. 2003. *The Fluent Reader: Oral Reading Strategies for Building Word Recognition, Fluency, and Comprehension*. New York: Scholastic.

———. 2006. Fluency: An Oft-Neglected Goal of the Reading Program. In *Understanding and Implementing Reading First Initiatives*, ed. C. Cummins, 60–71. Newark, DE: International Reading Association.

Wolf, Maryanne. 2005. *What is Fluency? Fluency Development: As the Bird Learns to Fly*. Scholastic professional paper. New York: ReadAbout. http://teacher.scholastic.com /products/fluencyformula/pdfs/What_is_Fluency.pdf (accessed June 8, 2007).

CONTENTS OF THE DIGITAL RESOURCE CD

Teacher Resources

Page	Document Title	Filename
4	Standards Correlations Chart	standards.pdf
6	Writing Rubric	writingrubric.pdf writingrubric.doc
7	Fluency Assessment	fluency.pdf
8	Diagnostic Assessment Directions	directions.pdf
10	Practice Page Item Analysis Days 1–3	pageitem1.pdf pageitem1.doc pageitem1.xls
11	Practice Page Item Analysis Days 4–5	pageitem2.pdf pageitem2.doc pageitem2.xls
12	Student Item Analysis Days 1–3	studentitem1.pdf studentitem1.doc studentitem1.xls
13	Student Item Analysis Days 4–5	studentitem2.pdf studentitem2.doc studentitem2.xls

CONTENTS OF THE DIGITAL RESOURCE CD *(cont.)*

Practice Pages

The six practice pages for each week are contained in each PDF. In order to print specific days, open the desired PDF and select the pages to print.

Pages	Week	Filename
15–20	Week 1	week1.pdf
21–26	Week 2	week2.pdf
27–32	Week 3	week3.pdf
33–38	Week 4	week4.pdf
39–44	Week 5	week5.pdf
45–50	Week 6	week6.pdf
51–56	Week 7	week7.pdf
57–62	Week 8	week8.pdf
63–68	Week 9	week9.pdf
69–74	Week 10	week10.pdf
75–80	Week 11	week11.pdf
81–86	Week 12	week12.pdf
87–92	Week 13	week13.pdf
93–98	Week 14	week14.pdf
99–104	Week 15	week15.pdf
105–110	Week 16	week16.pdf
111–116	Week 17	week17.pdf
117–122	Week 18	week18.pdf
123–128	Week 19	week19.pdf
129–134	Week 20	week20.pdf
135–140	Week 21	week21.pdf
141–146	Week 22	week22.pdf
147–152	Week 23	week23.pdf
153–158	Week 24	week24.pdf
159–164	Week 25	week25.pdf
165–170	Week 26	week26.pdf
171–176	Week 27	week27.pdf
177–182	Week 28	week28.pdf
183–188	Week 29	week29.pdf
189–194	Week 30	week30.pdf
195–200	Week 31	week31.pdf
201–206	Week 32	week32.pdf
207–212	Week 33	week33.pdf
213–218	Week 34	week34.pdf
219–224	Week 35	week35.pdf
225–230	Week 36	week36.pdf